Institute for the
History of Technology
& Industrial Archaeology
MONOGRAPH SERIES, VOLUME IV, 1997

D0139102

# Bridges Over Time:

*A Technological Context for the
Baltimore and Ohio Railroad Main
Stem at Harpers Ferry, West Virginia*

By Michael W. Caplinger

The MONOGRAPH SERIES is published by the Institute for the History of Technology and Industrial Archaeology at West Virginia University in cooperation with the National Park Service and West Virginia University Press.

The mission of the Department of the Interior is to protect and provide access to our nation's natural and cultural heritage and honor our trust responsibilities to tribes.

For information on this series, related research reports, and IHTIA newsletters, please write: IHTIA/PUBLICATIONS, P.O. BOX 6305, MORGANTOWN, WV 26506.

*Bridges Over Time: A Technological Context for the Baltimore and Ohio Railroad Main Stem at Harpers Ferry, West Virginia* is a publication of the Institute for the History of Technology and Industrial Archaeology at West Virginia University.

ISBN 1-885907-04-4

**Library of Congress Cataloging-in-Publication Data**

Caplinger, Michael.

*Bridges Over Time: A Technological Context for the Baltimore and Ohio Railroad Main Stem at Harpers Ferry, West Virginia* / by Michael W. Caplinger. p. cm. -- (Institute for the History of Technology & Industrial Archaeology monograph series ; v. 4)

Includes bibliographical references.

ISBN 1-885907-04-4

1. Railroad bridges--West Virginia--Harpers Ferry--History.

2. Railroad bridges--West Virginia--Harpers Ferry--Design and construction. 3. Baltimore and Ohio Railroad Company--History. 4. Civil engineers--Biography. 5. Harpers Ferry (W. Va.)--History--construction. I. West Virginia University. Institute for the History of Technology and Industrial Archaeology. II. Title. III. Series: Monograph series (West Virginia University. Institute for the History of Technology and Industrial Archaeology) ; v. 4. TG25.H37C36 1997

624'.2'0975499--dc21                                                                                        97-11526

CIP

# Contents

## Part Four: John Brown's Raid, the Civil War, and Post-War Rebuilding: 1859-1893

## Part Five: The 1894 Improvements

## Part Six: The 1931 Improvements, the Main Stem Today, and Final Thoughts

## Bibliography

# Acknowledgements

This project was carried out under the auspices of the Institute for the History of Technology and Industrial Archaeology (IHTIA), a part of the Eberly College of Arts and Sciences at West Virginia University, with funding provided through the Historic American Building Survey/Historic American Engineering Record (HABS/HAER), a division of the National Park Service. This monograph arose out of a general survey of significant industrial archaeology-related resources along the Baltimore and Ohio Railroad's original main stem. It would not have been possible without the guidance, input, and aid of numerous persons who deserve a generous thanks: Dr. Emory Kemp gave direction and unflagging support for this work; my colleagues at the Institute for the History of Technology and Industrial Archaeology who gave valuable assistance, especially Billy Joe Peyton, Lee Maddex, and Dr. Michael Workman for reviews, Kevin McClung, Danny Bonenberger, and John Nicely for delineation, Larry Sypolt for archival aid and reviews, Christine Peyton-Jones for layout and design, graduate students Scott Daley and Shelley Birdsong for their research assistance in the early phases of this project, and Carol Lones for secretarial duties; Tim Hensley, Vice President of West Virginia State Relations for CSX Transportation, provided a number of historic drawings; David Simmons (of the Ohio Historical Society) edited and greatly improved the original draft; Donald Duppee reviewed the final draft; at Harpers Ferry National Park, Bruce Noble, Frank Schultz-Depalo, and Nancy Hatcher made available their assistance at any time; historian John Hankey reviewed the manuscript and provided valuable input and support; and Ann Calhoun at the B&O Railroad Museum's Hayes T. Watkins Archive was very helpful. A special thanks to all those B&O historians whose past work laid the foundation for this monograph.

# Foreword

Harpers Ferry is well known for the contributions of its armory to early technological growth in the United States and also as the site of John Brown's raid which helped to precipitate the Civil War. Less well known is the town's crucial role in the nation's transportation history. Shortly after the beginning of construction on both the Chesapeake & Ohio Canal and the Baltimore & Ohio Railroad in 1828, these two aspiring players in America's industrial development fought for building space in the narrow gap at Harpers Ferry where the Potomac and the Shenandoah Rivers join together and burst through a small opening in the mountains. The railroad ultimately prevailed in this competition and became the major mover of freight and passengers between the middle Atlantic coast and the Ohio Valley. Because of Harpers Ferry's prime location on this critical railroad line, the town became the principal supply point for General Sheridan's Shenandoah Valley campaign which led to the defeat of the Confederacy in the Civil War.

The ability to successfully bridge the Potomac River at Harpers Ferry proved to be an essential asset in the railroad's ability to surpass the canal in the race to the Ohio Valley. Because Harpers Ferry occupied a key location in this race, it had long been a place where innovations in bridge design and technology were applied to the challenge of crossing the town's two rivers. These bridges provided a passage way to John Brown and his raiders and also offered an inviting target as they were repeatedly destroyed and rebuilt during the Civil War. The ravages of raging flood waters also played havoc with the bridges of Harpers Ferry.

Given the complex interplay of construction and destruction, the intricacies of Harpers Ferry bridge history have often been a source of confusion for those studying the area's transportation network. This confusion has largely been eliminated through the publication of Michael W. Caplinger's *Bridges Over Time: A Technological Context for the Baltimore and Ohio Railroad Main Stem at Harpers Ferry, West Virginia*. Michael has continued the tradition of fine work produced by West Virginia University's Institute for the History of Technology and Industrial Archaeology and, in the process, he has clarified the complex story surrounding the history of the Harpers Ferry bridges. In so doing, he has crafted a readable study that offers a valuable contribution to the transportation history literature of the Middle Atlantic region.

*-Bruce J. Noble, Jr.*
*Chief, Interpretation & Cultural Resources Management*
*Harpers Ferry National Historical Park*

# Preface

In the early 1830s, the small industrial town of Harpers Ferry, Virginia, (West Virginia after 1863) was becoming a crossroads for turnpikes, canals, and railroads. In particular, it found itself on the route of the Baltimore and Ohio (or B&O) Railroad, the first great railroad undertaken in the United States and one of the most historically significant engineering accomplishments of the nineteenth century. This monograph is intended for those with an interest, not only in railroads, but in the history of technology and industrial archaeology. It strives to place the B&O Railroad's physical evolution at Harpers Ferry into a broader historical context focusing on railroad bridges, as the confluence of the Potomac and Shenandoah rivers provides a stunning setting for a series of railroad bridges built here between 1836 and 1931. Indeed, in the history of engineering certain rivers have been epic tests for bridge-builders and, for a time, the Potomac River at Harpers Ferry was such a place. Through a series of often unlikely events, three of the nineteenth century's great bridge designers--Lewis Wernwag and Benjamin Latrobe Jr. during the 1830s and 1840s, and Wendel Bollman during the 1850s and 1860s-- built bridges for the B&O's Potomac crossing. With the addition of two more bridges to the site (one in 1894 and another in 1931) four different era's of bridge-truss technology are represented, encompassing the transition from wood, to iron, and finally to steel building materials. Thus, Harpers Ferry, already rich in history, presents the opportunity to discuss important aspects of early American transportation and civil engineering.

**Part One** is a broad-based review of the rise of trans-Appalachian transportation improvements in the early nineteenth century. It recounts the Baltimore and Ohio Railroad's formation and explains why the B&O (and the Chesapeake and Ohio Canal) came to Harpers Ferry in the first place. This section ends with the arrival of the railroad on the riverbank across town, and provides biographical sketches of the engineers entrusted with designing and erecting the new bridge, Benjamin Latrobe Jr. and Lewis Wernwag, respectively. **Part Two** looks at the advent of the wooden-truss railroad bridge in America, its relationship to the rise of professionalism in the civil engineering community, and the development of the B&O's first standard wooden-truss design--all trends which manifested themselves in the B&O's first Potomac bridge at Harpers Ferry. **Part Three** through **Part Six** focuses on the planning, construction, and evolution of the B&O's *main stem* (the company's term for its original Baltimore-to-Wheeling line) at Harpers Ferry from 1834 to the present. The history of these bridges is recounted in the context of wider trends in American bridge-building practices. This includes a biographical sketch of Wendel Bollman and description of the truss system which bears his name; chronicles John Brown's Raid and the destruction of the Civil War; recounts the rise of the postwar bridge-building industry; and discusses the development of modern trusses and steel-plate girders. Lastly, this section identifies significant remains of the main stem at Harpers Ferry that are readily visible today.

Treating the subject in this manner means that certain aspects of the B&O's history at Harpers Ferry can be mentioned only in passing. This monograph focuses solely on the B&O's main stem, not the line of the Winchester and Potomac Railroad, an early railroad which met the B&O at Harpers Ferry and was later incorporated into the B&O system. References to rolling stock, train operations, business affairs and track development are few, as this is not the primary purpose of this work, nor is it why Harpers Ferry is so significant to the broader history of railroad engineering. In this sense, the following work differs from most conventional railroad histories, but the result is a better understanding of the B&O's physical remains than would otherwise be possible. The historical significance of the B&O main stem, in combination with the convergence of many different events, personalities, and structures important in the history of technology, makes Harpers Ferry the logical choice for such a specific treatment.

# List of Illustrations

## Part Six

# PART ONE:

# Harpers Ferry--Ties to Early American Transportation Systems and the Arrival of the Baltimore and Ohio Railroad

## Harpers Ferry

Harpers Ferry, West Virginia, lies 50 miles northwest of Washington, D.C., and 82 miles west of Baltimore, Maryland, at the confluence of the Shenandoah River with the Potomac River. Here at the uniting of the two rivers, the waters flow east through a rocky cleft in the Blue Ridge, presenting a sight that has attracted visitors since its discovery. The events hosted by this small town--the rise of modern manufacturing processes, the Civil War, the founding of Storer College, but especially John Brown's Raid on October 17, 1859--make Harpers Ferry uniquely important to American history. Less often recognized is the importance of Harpers Ferry to early American transportation, for it was a gateway to the west for one of the most daring and significant internal improvements undertaken by the young nation--the Baltimore and Ohio Railroad.

The town's beginnings can be traced to the establishment of a ferry service here in the mid-1700s. It was named after one of its first inhabitants, John Harper, who purchased land between the rivers and took over the ferry in 1757. The town, which sprang to life at the base of a bluff separating the Potomac and Shenandoah rivers, owes its existence to the water power available for early industries; the fall of the rivers here can supply over 20 feet of head for waterwheels.[2] One of the largest industries to locate here was the federal armory and arsenal which opened in 1799. This was at the suggestion of George Washington, who knew the site from his travels along the Potomac as a young man. Harpers Ferry was remote

Figure 1-An 1803 print by W. Roberts, Esq., looking eastward down the Potomac Valley from the bluff above Harpers Ferry. The Potomac enters this scene from the left, the Shenandoah from the right. The buildings shown include, from left to right, the armory, "Harper House," and the arsenal. Early industries were attracted by the water power the rivers provide at this point. For transportation improvements, the gap was a gateway to the Potomac and Shenandoah Valleys.

from the sea, and above the Great Falls of the Potomac, and therefore safe from seaborne raiders. This factory was one of only two federal armories in the country at the time and went on to produce some of the seminal weapon designs of the nineteenth century. Aside from the armory there were numerous private sawmills, gristmills, and machine shops, making Harpers Ferry the industrial center of the Potomac Valley during the ante-bellum period.

## A Transportation Gateway

While traditional industries located at Harpers Ferry to tap into the water power,

*"Through that stupendous gateway, walled with precipitous rocks, we enter the great valley." --Harpers New Monthly Magazine, 1859.[1]*

the transportation industry looked to the Potomac and Shenandoah Valleys as natural highways. Beginning with Native Americans, the major waterways coursing down the eastern and western flanks of the Appalachian Mountains became established corridors for trade and travel, and throughout the East such river valleys later proved to be the logical routes for turnpikes, canals, and, finally, railroads. In the East, river navigation was limited by the steep approach to the Alleghenies--the highest summits of the Appalachian chain--from the eastern seaboard. On the western side of the Alleghenies the Ohio River and its numerous branches beckoned, at times navigable as far upstream as Brownsville, Pennsylvania. The Ohio provided access to the great Mississippi River system, together forming thousands of miles of navigable river ripe for trade and travel. The easiest portages over the Alleghenies were found at the heads of

major rivers, ensuring the importance of eastern river corridors like the Potomac Valley to transportation-related internal improvement projects.[3]

The displacement of Native Americans in the Ohio River region and the subsequent expansion of population and trade west of the mountains would come to influence the history of transportation at Harpers Ferry. The grain, meat, and staples of the west reaped high prices in eastern markets mostly as a result of transportation costs, as the Appalachians prevented direct east-west trade. Most western products floated down the Ohio or Mississippi Rivers to New Orleans where ocean-going vessels would carry the goods to cities on America's eastern seaboard or overseas. New Orleans, at the mouth of the giant Mississippi River system, benefitted most from the waterborne trade, and became the envy of east coast merchants.[4] The perfection of the steamboat in the early 1800s made travel upstream relatively easy for the first time and facilitated the rapid expansion of river-oriented trade. Ohio River towns such as Wheeling, (West) Virginia, and Pittsburgh, Pennsylvania, became commercial trading centers. In the East, however, rivers were navigable only short distances inland and the steamboat was less useful. The east coast city which could tap the Ohio and Mississippi River trade with the best transmontane transportation link, siphoning trade that was otherwise headed for New Orleans, stood to gain an instant advantage over its neighbors. This was the catalyst behind the ensuing drive to build transportation systems eastward from the coast and across the Allegheny summits to the western waters.[5]

An all-water link across the mountains between the east coast and the western waters was viewed as being most desirable, but the eastern rivers required substantial improvements first. The first real attempts at such internal improvements did not occur until after the Revolutionary War, when industrialization began to take hold in this country. Capital was scarce, and the banking systems, markets, and ur-

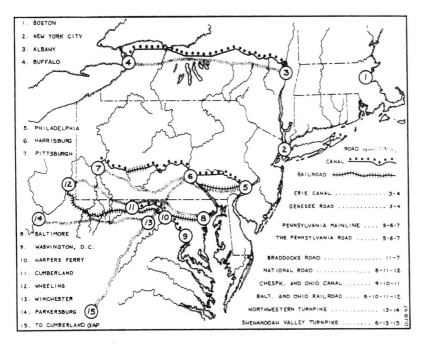

*Figure 2-In the East, the Appalachian Mountains proved to be a major barrier to direct east-west travel, trade and communication. As the United States developed, the westward-leading river corridors became focal points for transportation improvements to facilitate passage through this mountainous region to the Ohio and Mississippi River system. This map locates important cities and the routes of pioneering transportation improvements, including: the Erie Canal (top); the Pennsylvania Mainline, a hybrid canal, inclined plane system and railroad, (center); the National Road, Chesapeake and Ohio Canal, and Baltimore and Ohio Railroad (bottom). The crossing of the Alleghenies from the Potomac to the upper Ohio River system was the most difficult of the "portage" routes across the Eastern Continental Divide. (IHTIA, drawing by Daniel Bonenberger.)*

ban centers needed to support such works were, prior to 1800, only in their developmental stages. There was also a serious shortage of qualified engineers in the United States who were capable of organizing, designing, and carrying out large engineering projects; a situation which improved only slowly. Most of the planning and construction of America's earliest internal improvements were carried out by craftsmen--carpenters, blacksmiths, and machinists--aided by a smattering of formally trained engineers from Europe.

Even at this early time, Harpers Ferry found itself along one of the earliest major transportation improvements attempted in the United States, the ill-fated Potowmack Company. This company was chartered in 1786 to improve the Potomac and Shenandoah Rivers with locks and falls-skirting canals. The company improved the Shenandoah near Harpers Ferry at the beginning of the 1800s with hopes of opening the interior of Virginia, a dream only partially realized due to a lack of capital and the War of 1812. Other attempts and canal construction in the East were small in scope, and usually restricted to superficial river improvements.

The major port cities of the east, primarily New York, Philadelphia, Boston, Norfolk, and Baltimore were firmly entrenched as the centers of trade for their respective regions, and all had maintained a relative balance in economic development through the start of the 1800s. Each of these cities reaped the benefits of trade along the nearest westward-leading river valley. In a sense, each of the major eastern cities "claimed" a particular river as its corridor to the west. For New York City it was the Hudson and Mohawk River valleys which led across northern New York state to the Great Lakes; Philadelphia looked to the headwaters of the Susquehanna and Juanita Rivers in central Pennsylvania, which lay opposite the headwaters of the westward-flowing Allegheny River; farther south in Virginia the low passes lying between the James and

Kanawha Rivers offered a route to the west for Norfolk and Richmond.

Baltimore, Maryland, lying nearly equidistant between the mouths of the Potomac and Susquehanna, relied heavily on trade from the Potomac Valley. Due west from Baltimore, the Potomac River is reached after 70 miles at the Point of Rocks, 10 miles east (downriver) from Harpers Ferry. Upriver from Harpers Ferry the Potomac winds through sharp ridges to the foot of the Alleghenies and the city of Cumberland. West of Cumberland lie the headwaters of the Potomac, and across the Allegheny summits tributaries of the Monongahela and Youghigheny Rivers flowed west, giving access to various points on the middle and upper Ohio River. From Harpers Ferry the Shenandoah appeared equally appealing, providing access to the Great Valley of Virginia, and on to the Ohio via tributaries of the New, Kanawha, or Little Kanawha Rivers. Thus, Harpers Ferry was the gateway for transportation systems in both the upper Potomac and Shenandoah River valleys.

## The Race for the Western Waters

Turnpikes were the first really successful internal improvements of the trans-

*Figure 3-A depiction of a stagecoach on the National Road. As commerce increased in the Ohio and Mississippi River valleys, the need for better transportation links spurred grand construction projects in the form of turnpikes, canals, and finally railroads. (Painting by H.D. Stitt.)*

portation age. Roads across the mountains from the east coast first tapped the Ohio Valley trade in the 1750s, and helped maintain both Baltimore and Philadelphia as centers of trade in the east until the early 1820s. Throughout the East turnpike companies began linking towns into an ever-growing turnpike network. No less than three secondary turnpikes met at Harpers Ferry by the mid-1830s: the Harpers Ferry, Charlestown, and Smithfield Turnpike; the Frederick and Harpers Ferry Turnpike; and the Hillsborough and Harpers Ferry Turnpike. These connected Harpers Ferry to the primary turnpike road from Baltimore to Cumberland, which passed north of Harpers Ferry through Hagerstown.[6] From Cumberland, the National Road continued across the Alleghenies to the Ohio River at Wheeling (reaching that city in 1818), representing the greatest of the early turnpike roads. Turnpike wagons, however, could only carry small amounts of commodities and the costs of transport were high. Upkeep of the roadway was difficult as well. Turnpikes could not compete with the advantages of a canal moving materials in bulk, with much less effort and dramatically lower shipping costs.[7]

This race for the best east-west transportation link reached a new level in the early 1820s when businessmen and the state of New York built the nation's first great artificial waterway, the Erie Canal. Partially opened in 1823 and finished in 1825, the Erie Canal stretched 364 miles between Buffalo, N.Y., on Lake Erie, and Albany, N.Y., at the head of navigation on the Hudson River.[8] Goods immediately began flowing between Buffalo and New York City, and the canal was an unparalleled success. Even more enticing to eastern capitalists was the canals' tendency to stimulate growth all along its corridor, not just the extreme ends of the waterway. The Erie Canal's success in capturing the western trade and developing the region along its route, and the superior economic position it suddenly gave New York City, created panic among the business communities of all other eastern seaboard cities.

Consequently, a "canal craze" erupted as other cities sought to establish their own water connections to the west. In Baltimore, like other cities, near hysteria reigned amongst the business community, and the search for a solution to the "Erie problem" began.[9]

In reality, New York's Erie Canal benefitted from certain natural advantages. As a result, no other canal in the East would find similar success. The Baltimore tidewater was physically closer to the navigable midwestern rivers than New York City. Yet the Erie Canal, in crossing over to westward-flowing waters, had to surmount a summit level of 568 feet, while to the south the lowest passes confronting canals from Philadelphia or Baltimore averaged more than 2000 feet. The Hudson River provided a navigable passage through the highest Appalachian ridges for the first 200 miles to Albany. From Albany westward to Lake Erie, the landscape was long ago scoured nearly flat by glaciation. The Finger Lakes (also the result of glaciation) provided ample water for an artificial canal. To the south, the central Appalachians did not possess such beneficial natural conditions.

Despite these drawbacks, the other eastern cities had few options and plunged their resources into building canals westward with high hopes for economic success. Baltimore's closest rival, the state of Pennsylvania, began work in earnest on the "mainline" east-west improvement between Philadelphia and Pittsburgh (the Pennsylvania Mainline Canal connected the Schuylkill, Susquehanna, and Juanita Rivers with the Allegheny and Ohio Rivers by the mid-1830s with a hybrid canal, railroad, and inclined plane system). As it turned out, a water route to the west was out of the question for Baltimore, for the city did not sit directly along a suitable watercourse, and a canal connection to the Potomac River was prohibitively expensive. Besides, by 1825 the Chesapeake and Ohio (or C&O) Canal, a revitalized descendent of the old Patowmack Company, was planning to build along the Potomac (starting 25 miles south of Baltimore at Georgetown, across the river from Washington) and cross the Appalachians to the Ohio River. It appeared the benefits of an east-to-west canal link would never come directly to Baltimore.[10]

Finding itself with little chance for a suitable canal connection to the west, and its rivals working on grand canal projects of their own, Baltimore's leaders in 1827 boldly opted to throw their support behind a new kind of transportation system developing in Britain--the *railroad*. It meant big changes were in store for Harpers Ferry, as America's first great railroad, the Baltimore and Ohio, was soon advancing along the Potomac toward the little town.

## The Origins of the Baltimore and Ohio Railroad

After borrowing the basic idea of guided wagons from the mines of Germany, the British began building forerunners of the modern railroad, called *tramways*, around 1700. At first only used around coal mines or iron furnaces to haul minerals, tramways began to find success as feeder lines, supplying a variety of freight to Great Britain's growing canal system. After a century of technological experimentation and advancement, the British possessed an extensive system of horse-drawn tramways which they found to be as useful as canals for moving freight efficiently over long distances.[11] By the 1820s, nearly all of the essential components of modern railroads--metal rails, flanged wheels, track switches-- were in common use, and railroad construction began to explode in Britain.[12] At about the same time as the Erie Canal opened in this country, the British opened the world's first true railroads, establishing this new mode of transportation as a viable and practical alternative to canals. The success of the Stockton and Darlington, opened in 1825, and the Liverpool and Manchester, opened in 1830, and the fact that steam locomotives were proven to work well on these lines, provided stimulus for railroad construction

*Figure 4-The ceremonial laying of the B&O's "First Stone" on July 4, 1828. The B&O main stem marks the beginning of America's trunkline railroad system. (Painting by Stanley M. Arthurs.)*

worldwide. The citizens of Baltimore found inspiration in the British successes.

America had lagged a century behind Britain in canal construction, and two centuries in turnpike construction. This would not be the case with the railroad, as the United States adopted it directly on the heels of the British. In the fall of 1826, when the city of Baltimore despaired over the canal situation, Evan Thomas, brother of prominent Baltimore merchant Philip Thomas, returned from Great Britain. Evan had been impressed with Britain's railroads, and the two brothers began marshalling support for Baltimore's own. Word spread like fire, and Baltimore's business and political community seized upon the idea of a railroad to the Ohio River as the solution to their transportation dilemma.[13]

A group of twenty-five Baltimoreans, the company's founders, met formally twice over the winter of 1826-27 to discuss the possibilities of a railroad to the Ohio River, and "take into consideration the best means of restoring to the city of Baltimore that portion of the Western Trade which has lately been diverted from it by the introduction of steam navigation and by other causes."[14] Regarding railroads, the founders agreed that, "Indeed, so completely has this improvement succeeded in England, that it is the opinion of many judicious and practical men there, that these roads will, for heavy transportation, supersede canals as effectually as canals have superseded turnpike-roads."[15] Heavy loads could be drawn easier and faster, and unlike canals a railroad could operate in winter--a key advantage. The meetings culminated in the chartering of the Baltimore and Ohio Railroad, organized on April 23, 1827, with a capital stock of five million dollars.[16] The state legislatures of Maryland, Virginia, and Pennsylvania all chartered the company by 1828, making it the first common-carrier railroad in the country, and granted the B&O permission to begin construction on the main stem.[17] The goal would be Wheeling, nearly 400 miles to the west on the Ohio River.

Compared to the relatively well-known turnpike and canal systems, a new technological epoch was at hand in the United States when Baltimore's business leaders formed the Baltimore and Ohio Railroad. Deciding to build a railroad across the Appalachians was an incredibly daring move, as in reality few Americans could visualize exactly how a railroad would operate, or were sure they could compete successfully with canals. There

were only two well-known examples of horse or gravity-powered tramways in the United States in the mid-1820s, and none of America's handful of civil engineers had ever built a railroad like Baltimore proposed. In addition, the British had not built across any obstacle like the Appalachian Mountains, much less through 400 miles of densely forested wilderness. But the railroad promised to save Baltimore from economic ruin, and the citizens of that city were willing to back up their hopes with capital.

Jubilant crowds witnessed the ceremonial laying of the "first stone" of the B&O on July 4, 1828, thus beginning Baltimore's quest for the Ohio River. The esteemed James Carroll, the only surviving signer of the Declaration of Indpendence, turned the first spade of earth and pronounced this action to be equal, if not more important, than signing that famous document.[18] Ironically, in Georgetown on that same day dignitaries held a groundbreaking for the C&O Canal, with John Quincy Adams turning the first spadeful of earth. He struck a root, an ill omen for the canal's advance west. The B&O, like the C&O Canal, desired to pass through the narrows at Harpers Ferry. Incredibly Harpers Ferry found itself on the line of two of this country's most important internal improvements. One of them, the B&O Railroad, represented the cutting edge of Americanized railroad technology. When both the C&O and the B&O reached Harpers Ferry, there was still less than 1000 miles of railroad, and less than 2000 miles of canals, on the continent.[19]

## The B&O's First Years

The B&O constructed its line west from Baltimore to Wheeling in essentially three great surges over a twenty-five-year period.[20] The first of these began in 1828 and ended in 1834 at Harpers Ferry, 82 miles from Baltimore. Just reaching that point was more difficult than anyone anticipated. The B&O's original engineering corps, a combination of civilian and military engineers, quickly finished the initial reconnaissance surveys for a route

| Opened To: | Miles from Baltimore: | Date: |
|---|---|---|
| Ellicott Mills, Md. | 14 | May 24, 1830 |
| Monocacy, Md. | 61 | Dec. 1, 1831 |
| Point of Rocks, Md. | 69 | Apr. 1, 1832 |
| **Harpers Ferry, Va.** | **82** | **Dec. 1, 1834** |
| Martinsburg, Va. | 100 | May 4, 1842 |
| Cumberland, Md. | 170 | Nov. 5, 1842 |
| Wheeling, Va. | 373 | Jan. 3, 1853 |

*Figure 5-Opening dates for various points on the B&O main stem. Harpers Ferry marked the end of the first of three phases of construction. The main stem was the last of the pioneer east-west trunkline railroads to reach the western waters when completed to Wheeling.*

from Baltimore to the Potomac. They were led by Jonathan Knight and military engineer Lt. Colonel Stephen Long, who reported their findings on April 5, 1828. They chose a route from Baltimore to the Patapsco River at Relay, Maryland (far above that river's mouth on the Chesapeake Bay because of a political compromise with downtown Baltimore merchants), and thence following the Patapsco and Monocacy Rivers to the Potomac River at Point of Rocks, Maryland.[21] Consequently, "The road was accordingly promptly located along this line, and the necessary titles were acquired to the land upon almost the whole of the section bordering of the Potomac River."[22]

Once construction began in 1828, B&O officials found out that building to the Ohio would take considerably longer than the five years that some optimistically hoped. Delays and disagreements among the engineers and board of directors, and unexpected construction problems, were the main culprits. (These are discussed in Part Two.) Indeed, there were differences in opinion on every facet of the new line. Slowly, contractors graded the right-of-way and built bridges, and a twin set of tracks stretched out from Baltimore. With no immediate source for locomotives, and wanting to open the road quickly, the company decided to use horse power. The first horse-drawn car departed for Ellicott's Mills--13 miles west of the B&O's main shops at Mount Clare in west Baltimore--on May 22, 1830. The company faced the sobering realization that at the current rate of construction it would take forty years to reach the Ohio River.[23] Not surprisingly, the original estimates of the time and money required to build the railroad were woefully inadequate, and monetary difficulties would thereafter plague the line's westward advance.

## Approaching Harpers Ferry: The Point of Rocks-C&O Canal Dispute

The line opened to Point of Rocks, on the Potomac River 72 miles from Baltimore, on April 1, 1832. At this spot, the C&O Canal and the B&O Railroad came into direct conflict for the first time. For 12 miles from Point of Rocks to Harpers Ferry the shoreline of the Potomac is reduced to a mere sliver of land. In some sections the projected routes for the two works overlapped, forcing the rival companies into a court battle over the right-of-way through the narrows. The situation was complicated by the existence of the Harpers Ferry to Frederick Turnpike on the same shore. The legal conflict actually began in 1829 when the canal company obtained an injunction to stop the railroad from acquiring land in the narrows. The railroad reciprocated and construction of both works stopped at Point of Rocks. B&O historian William Prescott Smith later wrote, "This controversy, although supposed at the time to be likely to cause no delay in the construction of the work, proved by subsequent experience to be a barrier as difficult to overcome as the ridges of the Alleghenies."[24]

While stalled at Point of Rocks, the B&O's engineers turned to constructing a 25-mile-long branch line from Baltimore to Washington, D.C., which opened July 20, 1835. It was the first railroad to enter the nation's capital. Also, during the delay steam locomotives came into regular use, steadily replacing horse power. The first locomotives on the B&O were known as "Grasshopper" engines (weighing just eight tons) and made their operational appearance on the B&O in 1831. By 1834, steam locomotives operated regularly over the railroad between Baltimore and Point of Rocks.

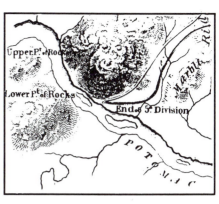

*Figure 6-The B&O's first serious setback came at Point of Rocks, Maryland. Here the B&O reached the Potomac's north shore and immediately became embroiled in litigation with the C&O Canal, which was also nearing Point of Rocks, over the right-of-way through the narrows between Point of Rocks and Harpers Ferry. (From the Baltimore & Ohio Railroad Fifth Annual Report, 1831.)*

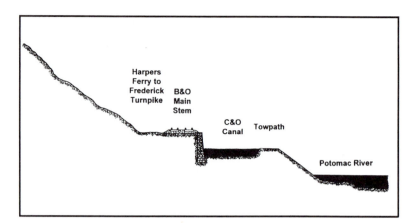

*Figure 7-When construction through the narrows downstream of Harpers Ferry resumed in 1834, the turnpike, railroad and canal were squeezed onto the Potomac's north shore. At certain points, lack of space (and the canal compromise) forced the railroad to build masonry retaining walls to carry the turnpike and main stem along the inner bank of the C&O Canal. This cross section shows the configuration of the three works just downriver from Harpers Ferry. (IHTIA, drawing by author.)*

The canal/railroad legal dispute grew more rancorous, and finally landed in a Maryland legislative arbitration committee, which produced recommendations quite favorable to the canal company in early 1833. Both companies accepted the decision and entered into a period of tenuous, though genuine, cooperation. The railroad agreed to: cooperate in locating the line through the narrows; convey railcars through the narrows by horse power so as not to scare the barge tow animals; erect a board fence to separate the two works; build retaining walls where needed in the narrows to support the railroad along the inner bank of the canal; recognize the canal's right to the north bank of the Potomac above Harpers Ferry; and, halt construction west of Harpers Ferry until the C&O canal reached Cumberland (which the railroad hoped would not take long) or until the canal's current charter expired in 1840. The B&O paid the canal company to build both canal and railroad--and relocate the Frederick Turnpike--through the worst parts of the narrows, and agreed to support the canal in their efforts to reach Cumberland.[25] The 1833 settlement with the canal company left the B&O with little choice but to wait for years while the canal company continued building toward Cumberland.

## Arrival of the B&O Railroad on the Riverbank Opposite Harpers Ferry

An especially disheartening result of the canal agreement was the B&O's exclusion from the Potomac's north shore all the way to Cumberland. This meant the B&O had to cross the Potomac at Harpers Ferry, or be forced to turn north toward Hagerstown at Point of Rocks and bypass Harpers Ferry altogether. Additionally, many segments of the Potomac's south shore upstream from Harpers Ferry are lined with rocky, overhanging bluffs, requiring extensive work to make room for the railroad. But the prospect of an immediate connection with the new Winchester and Potomac (W&P) Railroad, then building north from Winchester, Virginia, along the Shenandoah to Harpers Ferry, was too much to pass up. A connection with this new 30-mile line, which reached Harpers Ferry in 1836, would immediately bring goods from the fertile Shenandoah Valley. It also held the promise of further extensions south into Virginia. The board envisioned the W&P as "virtually a prolongation of the Baltimore and Ohio Railroad up the valley of the Shenandoah."[26] After the canal compromise, the primary concern was reaching Harpers Ferry and connecting with the Winchester and Potomac.

In early 1834, Benjamin H. Latrobe Jr. (the B&O's new engineer of location) and the canal company engineers finalized the dual routes through the narrows downstream between Harpers Ferry and Point of Rocks. On December 1, 1834, the B&O's tracks officially opened to the riverbank opposite Harpers Ferry, below the rocky cliffs known as Maryland Heights. It stopped at the east end of a turnpike bridge known as Wager's bridge. The *Virginia Free Press* in Martinsburg reported:

> Harpers-Ferry presents a busy scene since the extension of the rail road. The narrow strip of ground at the northern termination of the [Wager] bridge is crowded with commodities, wagons, drays and spectators. And the long trains for burthen [sic] cars, resembling small huts in their structure, seem like so many villages imbued with locomotion. The travelling from Harpers-Ferry to Baltimore is said to average thirty passengers daily; and an average of

five hundred barrels of flour, besides other articles of produce, is dispatched every day from the Ferry to Baltimore.[27]

The circumstances at Harpers Ferry--two major rivers, a general lack of space, the desire to connect with the Winchester and Potomac Railroad, and the need to accommodate both the Harpers Ferry and Frederick Turnpike *and* the C&O Canal--combined to make a complicated situation for the B&O's engineers.

## The Potomac Barrier and Wager's Bridge

By the end of 1834, the B&O's earlier plans of holding to the Potomac's north bank the entire distance to Cumberland appeared impossible. So while the canal continued on, the railroad was crammed onto the foot of the cliffs across from town. The B&O would have to cross the river here to connect with the Winchester and Potomac Railroad, the best the railroad could hope for.

Bridging the Potomac River at this spot was not a simple matter. It was the widest river crossing the B&O faced on the main stem. Above Harpers Ferry, the Potomac averages some 1200 feet in width, but narrows to under 900 feet as it approaches the Shenandoah. The river is subject to severe floods that can raise the water level 30 feet with little warning. During dry seasons, the Potomac averages 5 feet or less in depth, but storms on the slopes of the Alleghenies can quickly swell the river in the confined passage at Harpers Ferry.[28] The Shenandoah River can be equally severe, and floods are particularly destructive at the confluence of the two rivers. Torrents often swept through the homes, businesses, and factories in low-lying Harpers Ferry and on Virginius Island. Any bridge here was extremely vulnerable.

At first, Knight and Latrobe considered laying the line across Wager's toll bridge. It was owned by the Wager family--descendants of Robert Harper--who also owned the shoreline approaches on either side of the river. Wager's bridge had

## Lewis W. Wernwag: A Biographical Sketch

Lewis William Wernwag (1769-1843) was one of the preeminent bridge builders in America during the first half of the nineteenth century.[33] After emigrating from Germany to America at the age of seventeen, he found success as a mechanic and carpenter--building mills, waterwheels, and related machinery--before designing his first bridge at the age of forty-one. Using intuition and traditional methods he stretched the structural limits of wood spans, and his arched and cantilevered trusses were soon among the longest wood spans in the world. He built as many as thirty bridges in Pennsylvania, Delaware, Maryland, Virginia, Kentucky, and Ohio between 1810 and 1836.[34] Wernwag constructed his most well-known span--the 340 foot-long "Colossus"--in 1812 over the Schuylkill River at Philadelphia.[35] It was the longest single-span bridge built in America up to that time, and it made Wernwag a highly sought-after contractor.

From about 1813 to 1818, Wernwag lived and worked at Phoenixville, Pennsylvania, along the Schuylkill River, and moved in 1819 to Conowingo, Maryland, on the Susquehanna River. He left a trail of monumental wooden bridges in his wake. Wernwag originally came to Harpers Ferry in 1824 to work on Wager's Bridge, the first to cross the Potomac at this point. Wernwag and his sons took up residence at Harpers Ferry on Virginius Island and opened a water-powered sawmill. He built a three-story machine shop in 1832 near his sawmill, and for years presided over the small industrial complex. Wernwag was a tinkerer, and could build nearly anything using the assortment of lathes and milling equipment in his machine shop. He managed the business on the island for nine years, and sold it to his son. Wernwag built a number of other structures in the area, and also rebuilt the government dam which diverted water from the Potomac into the armory's power canal. He is credited with building the first wooden railroad bridge in the United States in 1831 at the B&O's Monocacy River crossing east of Harpers Ferry.

Wernwag's bridge-truss systems were among the earliest patented bridge trusses in the United States. He received his first patent in 1812 while living in Phoenixville, and his second in 1829 while living at Harpers Ferry, but he also built other truss types. Wernwag's bridges generally performed well, although he--like other self-taught bridge builders at the time--had no formal way of computing the stresses at work in individual members. Wernwag reflected the artisan tradition, a fact which will be discussed further in Part Two. While the sawmills Wernwag routinely opened wherever he lived were essential to his bridge-building success, his most groundbreaking efforts were in the incorporation of iron components into his spans. "Wernwag's practice was to saw all his timbers through the heart, to detect unsound wood and permit good seasoning of the timbers. He used no timbers of a greater thickness than 6 inches, and separated all the sticks of his arches by cast washers, to allow free circulation of the air."[36] He used iron in ways other than cast washers--his use of wrought-iron diagonals on a bridge over the Delaware River at New Hope, Pennsylvania, in 1813-1814 marks "the first step in America in the long series of experiments that eventually led to the all-iron truss."[37] Wernwag's two bridges at Harpers Ferry were among his last great construction projects before his death there on August 12, 1843.

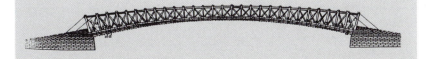

*Figure 8-Wernwag's bridge truss patented in 1829. (From Wernwag, **Truss Bridge**, U.S. Patent Number 5760x, December 22, 1829.)*

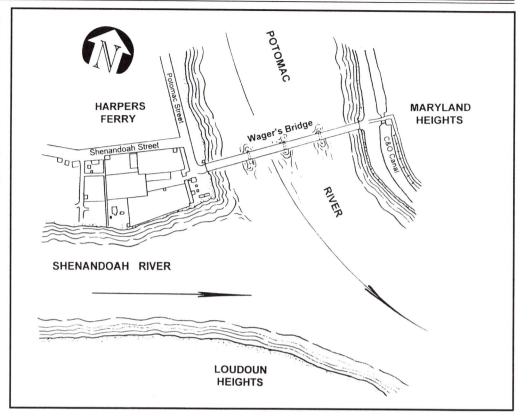

*Figure 9-A map showing Wager's turnpike bridge at Harpers Ferry in 1834. Lewis Wernwag built this bridge in the mid-1820s, and the B&O considered laying tracks across it before opting for its own crossing in 1835. Wernwag was one of the most well-known bridge builders in America at the time, and a trusted B&O contractor. (IHTIA, drawing by author.)*

# Benjamin H. Latrobe Jr.: A Biographical Sketch

*Figure 10-Benjamin H. Latrobe Jr., ca. 1855.*

The new bridge's designer, Benjamin H. Latrobe Jr. (1806-1878) was destined for fame greater than Wernwag's. Latrobe was an up-and-coming civil engineer in 1834, still just learning the finer points of the profession. His father, Benjamin H. Latrobe Sr. (1764-1820), was educated in the great architecture and engineering schools of Europe, and in 1795 immigrated from England to America. The elder Latrobe became America's foremost architect and engineer, designing such lasting landmarks as the Fairmount Waterworks in Philadelphia and portions of the Capitol building in Washington after its destruction in the War of 1812. Benjamin Latrobe Jr. and his older brother, John H.B. Latrobe (1803-1891), were trained at schools in Washington and Baltimore, and by their father. Benjamin Jr. first tried law, and for a while practiced in Baltimore with his brother's firm. However, he soon left for New Jersey where he "learned something about timber and surveying" while acting as agent for a tract of land owned by his mother and uncle.[38]

In 1830 Benjamin Latrobe Jr. returned to Baltimore, where his brother now handled legal affairs for the new railroad. In July 1830 John helped get Benjamin a job as an assistant on a survey crew along the B&O main stem west of Ellicott Mills, Maryland. Latrobe was not formally schooled in the field of engineering, but his grasp of mathematics (and no doubt family ties) helped him attain the position, and he quickly began schooling himself in the finer points of architecture and engineering. His brother later commented, "It was a swap between us. I had been educated as an engineer and became a lawyer, and he, educated as a lawyer, became an engineer."[39] Chief Engineer Jonathan Knight quickly elevated Latrobe to the position of assistant engineer, and his responsibilities expanded steadily through the early 1830s. His meteoric rise through the ranks was aided by the fact that there were so few professional engineers available in the United States at the time.

In 1831 Knight related that Latrobe was employed as his assistant, "superintending the laying of the railway" on both the second and fifth division, surveying and staking out the center line of the road in preparation for laying the rail.[40] In 1833 Latrobe was twenty-six years old and had worked for the company only three years when Jonathan Knight asked him to play a major role in the route surveys for the B&O's new Washington Branch. As part of his work on the Washington Branch he designed and oversaw construction of his first bridge, the Thomas Viaduct at Relay, Maryland--the largest masonry viaduct in the New World when completed in 1834.

been built between 1824 and 1826 by Lewis Wernwag, a famous contractor and bridge builder living in Harpers Ferry. The railroad had built to this point evidently thinking Wager's Bridge might be used to carry the line across the river and into Harpers Ferry.[29]

Wager's bridge consisted of four wooden spans (each about 200 feet long) of unknown truss design, carrying two lanes of highway, totalling approximately 800 feet from abutment to abutment.[30] The spans rested on three mid-river piers of coarse stone. With the arrival of the C&O Canal, a fifth span was added to the bridge's east end to cross over the C&O Canal basin to a new abutment. The abutment sat at the foot of Maryland Heights and left no room for any sort of curvature at the base of the bluff; the turnpike literally made a 90-degree turn to get onto the bridge. The west end of the bridge reached the Virginia shore among the buildings of lower Harpers Ferry.

Engineers from the B&O, the C&O Canal, and the Winchester and Potomac Railroad conferred on Wager's bridge. In addition to the impossible turn at the east entrance to the bridge, the engineers concluded the structure was in poor condition and needed extensive work before it could carry trains. Since Wager was demanding compensation to use his inadequate bridge, the B&O decided to build its own structure, estimated to cost $85,000 on a new and better alignment.[31] Chief Engineer Jonathan Knight gave the job designing the new bridge to Benjamin Latrobe Jr., and hired Lewis Wernwag to erect it.[32] These two men, and the bridge they built, are of considerable significance to the broader history of technology and engineering in the nineteenth century. Therefore, contextual background on certain biographical, technological, and engineering points must be reviewed to fully gauge the importance of the B&O's first Harpers Ferry bridge.

When the B&O continued west from Point of Rocks in 1834, Latrobe was put in charge of locating the railroad, working with canal company engineers to locate the line through the narrows. After designing the Harpers Ferry bridge, he temporarily left the B&O for a year to work on the Baltimore and Port Deposit Railroad.[41] Construction began on the Harpers Ferry bridge in late 1835 without Latrobe supervising, and it would not be finished until early 1837.

Latrobe returned to the B&O in mid-1836, and this time he would remain with the company nearly twenty years. He soon eclipsed Jonathan Knight, becoming the guiding light of the B&O's engineering department, supervising the continuation of the B&O to Cumberland in 1842. Jonathan Knight retired that year, and Latrobe became chief engineer. He was an all-around builder, designing bridges, tunnels, and many other types of structures. Latrobe was already one of the most well-known civil engineers in America when, during 1848-1853, he supervised the completion of the B&O's original main stem to Wheeling, finally fulfilling Baltimore's dream of a link to the west. The completed main stem was widely considered as one of the greatest civil engineering feats of the ante-bellum period. It was also a trial run for the eventual crossing of the Rockies, and viewed around the world as a case study for railroad construction through mountainous territory. Latrobe's acceptance of steep gradients on the B&O's main stem over the Alleghenies, up to 116 feet per mile, later led to the adoption of 116 feet per mile as the maximum allowable grade on the transcontinental railroads crossing the Rockies.

Besides the Thomas Viaduct, a masonry structure, Latrobe built numerous wooden bridges on the B&O. But as a bridge truss designer Latrobe was only partially successful, experimenting with different forms of trusses through the years but never patenting a particular truss system. Most of the bridges he built on the B&O followed the style of his bridge at Harpers Ferry, a relatively obscure truss design later termed the Latrobian truss (described in Part Two), notable more for its resemblance to a famous European truss and its uncommon incorporation of iron components than as a widely used truss layout. Latrobe avidly supported using wrought and cast iron as integral components in bridges (and all other structures) at a time when many engineers still distrusted the material. Under his tutelage in the 1840s and early 1850s, B&O employees Albert Fink and Wendel Bollman developed into world-class bridge engineers. Latrobe put their skills with iron to use in crossing the Alleghenies, and both Fink and Bollman patented successful all-iron bridge trusses.

Ironically, Latrobe is known more for his tunnel building and acceptance of high gradients than his own bridge designs. He designed the 4100-foot-long Kingwood Tunnel, the longest railroad tunnel in the country when opened in 1852, and over forty additional tunnels on the B&O's lines.[42] After leaving the B&O upon the completion of the main stem in 1853, Latrobe acted as chief engineer for the construction of two B&O branch lines--the Northwestern Virginia Railroad, and the Pittsburgh & Connellsville Railroad. He later worked as a private consultant on projects including the Hoosac Tunnel and the Brooklyn Bridge before finally retiring in 1875. Aside from his pure engineering works, Latrobe originated the railroad unit of work measurement, the "ton-mile," and also endorsed the laying of the world's first Morse telegraph line along the B&O's Washington Branch.[43] Benjamin Latrobe Jr. died in Baltimore on October 19, 1878.

## Notes

1. Anonymous, "Artists' Excursion on the Baltimore and Ohio Rail Road," 8.

2. Gilbert, *Where Industry Failed...*, 6.

3. Rubin, *Canal or Railroad?, 5-9.*

4. Savage, *An Economic History of Transportation*, 177.

5. Ibid.

6. Gilbert, 5.

7. Rubin, 70.

8. Kirby, *Engineering in History*, 216.

9. Rubin, 70.

10. Rubin, 65-68.

11. Savage, 181.

12. Smith, *The Book of the Great Railway Celebrations of 1857*, 8.

13. Ibid, 6-7.

14. Ibid, 6.

15. Ibid, 8.

16. Ibid, 10.

17. Ibid, 11.

18. Ibid, 13.

19. Baer, *Canals and Railroads of the Mid-Atlantic States, 1800-1860*, 35.

20. Smith, *History and Description of the Baltimore and Ohio Railroad*, 98.

21. Harwood, *Impossible Challenge, The Baltimore and Ohio Railroad in Maryland*, 11.

22. Smith, 13.

23. Harwood, 21.

24. Smith, 13.

25. Dilts, *The Great Road*, 118-120.

26. *Baltimore and Ohio Railroad Tenth Annual Report*, 1836, 3.

27. *Virginia Free Press*, December, 1834, 3.

28. Sisson, "Harpers Ferry Improvement," 351.

29. Dilts,191.

30. Snell, "Historic Building Site Survey Report for Wager Lot No. 1 and the Bridge Lot...," 16.

31. Dilts, 192.

32. *Baltimore and Ohio Railroad Ninth Annual Report, 1835*, 23.

33. Plowden, *Bridges, The Spans of North America*, 37.

34. Tyrell, *History of Bridge Engineering*, 136.

35. Plowden, 36.

36. Cooper, "American Railroad Bridges," 8.

37. Condit, *American Building Art: The Nineteenth Century*, 87.

38. Dilts, 160.

39. Ibid.

40. *Baltimore and Ohio Railroad Fifth Annual Report*, 1831, 16.

41. Smith, 31.

42. Drinker, *Tunneling, Explosive Compounds, and Rock Drills*, 28.

43. Lee, *A Biographical Dictionary of American Engineers*, 80.

# PART TWO

# The Advent of Wooden-Truss Railroad Bridges, Conflicts in the Civil Engineering Community, and the Related Significance of the B&O's Potomac Bridge

## The Advent of Wooden-Truss Railroad Bridges

Much of the importance of the B&O's Harpers Ferry bridge stems from its construction during a pivotal time in American civil engineering. This was the age of the wooden covered bridge, but the true significance behind these bridges lie in the truss system underneath the protective wooden covering. The truss, a structural form based on the rigid triangle, was a very important development in the history of technology and civil engineering. The simplest forms of trusses, such as the king-post or queenpost trusses, had been used in roof systems and for very short bridges for hundreds of years, but bridge trusses remained largely undeveloped until the Renaissance and the work of Palladio and Leonardo DeVinci. Long-span wooden trusses were a new alternative to the timber pile-and-beam bridge (which had only short, log-length spans) and the masonry arch (a strong but costly structure). Beginning around 1800 in the United States, new roads and turnpikes--in combination with the wide availability of timber and the high cost of labor required on masonry bridges--began pushing the development of long-span wooden trusses. Longer spans also meant fewer piers, and less hinderance to navigation.

Early American bridge builders such as Timothy Palmer, Theodore Burr, and Lewis Wernwag began creating new truss designs, slowly increasing the strength and length of wooden bridges. They devised a variety of truss systems, each having certain advantages and disadvantages relating to difficulty of erection, possible length of span, strength, and cost. Many nineteenth century bridge-builders patented their own truss system (which was usually named after the inventor), using it on their projects and licensing other builders to use the layout. A few early forms (such as the Burr arch, or Town lattice trusses) were very successful in their all-wooden form, but most others lacked any real promise of widespread usage and eventually faded away. Development of these early truss systems was largely by trial and error, with little in the way of structural theory to aid master carpenters instinctively rearranging the various truss members into new patterns. While the truss layouts differed among these builders, wooden arches were always incorporated into spans over 100 feet to supplement the trusses. The type of truss used

> "A man of my age that carried on extensive business for thirty-five years, and all of the knowlege & experience that I am at this time in possession of, I have not got from theory, but from severe knocks on my knuckles." --Lewis Wernwag, 1830.[1]

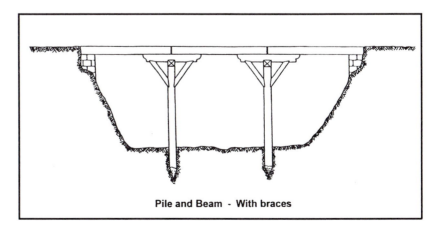

**Pile and Beam - With braces**

*Figure 1-For centuries, wooden bridges were of pile-and-beam construction. Their short, low spans restricted navigation, but they were relatively simple to erect across waterways. (IHTIA, drawing by author.)*

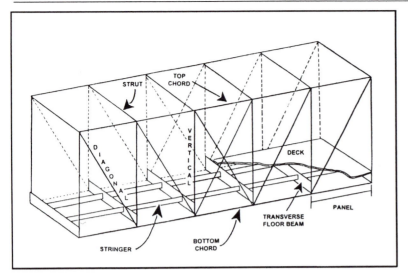

*Figure 2-This illustration identifies basic parts of a bridge truss. The various structural members forming a truss can be dividing into two basic categories: those which undergo tensile (pulling) forces, and those which undergo compressive (crushing) forces. These structural members can be arranged in a variety of ways, but only a few layouts combine the qualities of practicality, strength, easy erection, efficient and economic use of material and safety. Regardless of their configuration or material composition, all trusses have one thing in common: they are structural systems to transfer a load, and the weight of the truss itself, to either end of the truss, and then vertically down into stone piers or abutments. The example here is a basic Pratt truss, patented in 1842. (IHTIA, drawing by author.)*

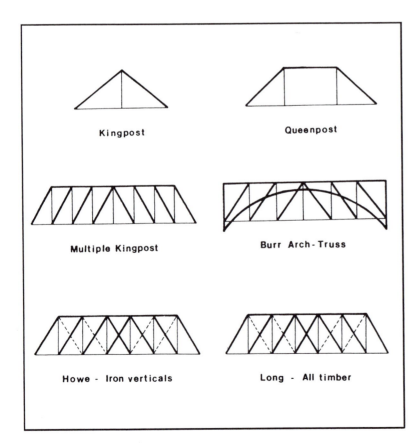

*Figure 3-Six successful, early wooden-truss layouts. The Kingpost (pre-1700), Queenpost (pre-1700), multiple Kingpost (ca. 1790), the Burr arch (ca. 1812), Long truss (ca. 1831), and Howe truss, (1840). (IHTIA, drawing by John Nicely.)*

at a particular place was largely up to the builder, who usually tried to choose the optimum design for the given situation.

Such wooden bridges were a mainstay of early turnpike roads. The lower cost and ease of constructing wooden-truss bridges, combined with the notable successes of builders like Wernwag, made them increasingly popular for crossing even major watercourses. But wooden bridges had serious drawbacks which were particularly disheartening for railroad engineers, namely, susceptibility to fire, decay from the effects of weather, and a definite ceiling on their carrying capacity as the weight of railroad rolling stock increased. Wooden spans were constantly being improved, and even before the advent of railroads builders began incorporating cast- and wrought-iron features to strengthen their structures. These hybrid wood-and-iron trusses were the precursors to the all-iron truss.

In the early 1830s the uncertainty of railroad loadings and long-term use left even veteran wooden-bridge builders apprehensive about using timber in lieu of masonry arch viaducts, and many disagreements ensued. This wood versus masonry dichotomy arose at a time of change in the professional engineering (and railroad) community in general. This inter-related transition is vividly illustrated by the dispute which arose among the B&O's engineers while building the line to Harpers Ferry, culminating in construction of the Potomac River bridge.

## The Rise of Professionalism in the Engineering Community and the B&O's "Stone Versus Wood" Debate, 1828-1834

This was an evolutionary period for the civil engineering profession in America, encompassing the somewhat antagonistic changeover from traditional "carpenter engineers"--like Wernwag--to native-born, highly trained professionals--like Benjamin Latrobe Jr.[2] Formally trained civil engineers were scarce in the early 1800s, and most pioneering turnpikes, canals, and railroads relied on the limited number of engineers trained at the nation's only major school of civil engineering, the U.S. Military Academy at West Point, founded in 1802. These military engineers, increasingly loaned out for civilian projects, were the catalyst for professionalization of the engineering field, dooming men like Wernwag and opening the way for engineers like Latrobe. This was facilitated by the General Survey Act of 1824, which officially authorized military engineers to aid civil works projects.

As touched upon in Part One, from 1828 to 1830 the B&O relied on a combination of military and civilian engineers. The army officers were led by the prestigious Lt. Col. Long, an accomplished engineer and explorer. The military engineers were balanced by two civilians, Jonathan Knight and Casper Wever. Knight was a self-taught engineer (and Pennsylvania politician) with experience laying out part of the National Road in Pennsylvania and Ohio.[3] Knight brought along another Pennsylvanian, Wever, also an experienced contractor, mason, and superintendent on the National Road. Initially, the engineering department operated under a "board of engineers" consisting of Long, Knight, and B&O president Philip Thomas. Under the leadership of Long and Knight, the engineering staff planned the characteristics of the original 82 miles of railroad.

The old order, the carpenter engineers such as Knight, Wever, and Wernwag, relied more on traditional craft techniques and "rules of thumb" instead of mathematical analysis. The highly educated engineers of the U.S. Army, attentive to detail and proficient in the complicated mathematical formulae needed for scientific railroad design, represented a new order. Animosity between the two groups often boiled over, fueled by the fact that the B&O's engineers, like all those in the country, had no direct experience in designing a railroad. There were many differences in

opinion. Within the B&O two subjects sparked a major dispute: the types of bridges the railroad should build, and the freewheeling, sometimes unsound, engineering and business practices of Casper Wever. It was an epic battle between two different eras of engineering.[4]

Prior to 1830, when the line was still in its early planning and construction stages, Long had advocated the use of scientifically designed timber-truss bridges and he had devised a wooden truss suitable for railroads. Long reasoned that these types of inexpensive, easy-to-erect bridges were exactly what the country's railroads needed to cross America's great expanse. Considering the number of bridges that the B&O would need before reaching the Ohio River, wooden trusses were really the only logical, economically feasible design. The B&O's superintendent of construction, Wever opposed Long, arguing for the use of monumental masonry arches such as he had previously erected on the National Road. Wever, Knight, and the traditionalists did not trust wooden trusses to withstand the shock and weight of fast-moving, heavily loaded railroad cars. Besides, in imitation of British construction practices, Wever and Knight felt the B&O should erect viaducts of stone or brick. The term *permanent way* was commonly used in discussing railroads, and at first it was taken literally. The B&O's leaders considered it the "work of the age," and the permanency of stone would ensure its place in history.

Other conflicts erupted, mainly between Wever and Long. In the fall of 1828, Jonathan Knight and president Thomas left on a three-month trip to England to study railroads, leaving Long as the senior engineer in charge (or so he thought). To his shock, Long found Wever changing his bridge designs, or disregarding them altogether, and committing the cardinal sin of changing the railroad's location without higher approval. Long also felt that Wever had misused construction funds, and that

*Figure 4-The decision to build stone viaducts in leiu of wooden bridges cost the B&O much needed time and money in its advance west. The Carrollton Viaduct over Gwynns Falls in Baltimore, shown here, was built in 1829 and is the oldest railroad viaduct in America. Its 80-foot span can carry the heaviest modern locomotives. At such crossings Colonel Long advocated wooden structures, but the B&O's board of directors sided with Wever and the permanancy of stone.*

many expenditures could not be fully accounted. Wever considered himself the field supervisor, with the prerogative to change plans or locations. Denying any misuse of funds, he considered Long a "nit-picker" who worried over inconsequential details of little import to the construction.[5]

This personal discord coincided with the debate over timber versus masonry bridges, and the B&O's engineers were nearly at each others throats. Upon the return of Knight and Thomas from England in May of 1829, they threw their support behind Wever. Knight and Thomas were accustomed to the traditional engineer like Wever, who, while perhaps rough in methods, had proven capable of constructing a railroad. B&O officials considered him a loyal company employee simply doing his job. William McNeill, newly appointed as a fourth member of the board of engineers (and also a military engineer), agreed with Long's assessment of Wever. The two army engineers attempted to establish a more rational engineering system with a clearly identified chief engineer having tighter control on construction. The conflict reached its height in late 1829 when Long and McNeill brought formal complaints against Wever for unprofessional conduct.

Meanwhile Lewis Wernwag had become a trusted confidant to B&O president Thomas. Although Wernwag was not an employee, he was a respected engi-

neering figure, and Thomas asked his opinion on Long's timber bridges. Putting little confidence in the military engineer's mathematical talents, Wernwag backed Wever and masonry viaducts. Wernwag wrote Thomas:

> I have handled all those tools for many years, from a crow bar to a moulding plane, to be at the eleventh hour of my days under the control of engineers, as they are called.... I have forgot that they are before me in calculating. They may do it quicker to know how many cubic yeards [sic] it would take out of a hill to fill a hole but not in anything else.... Col. Long has always been very friendly towards me. I do not want his ill will, but I know if he puts up as many bridges as I have and standing as long as I have without any expense, then I will shake hands with him on even ground and not before.[6]

The B&O's board of directors exonerated Wever in December 1829. The following January, the board of engineers was abolished and Knight became chief engineer and Wever the superintendent of construction. Long left immediately, followed by McNeill, and both moved on to have successful careers (Long also became involved with river improvements west of the Appalachians). Long did have one chance to build a wooden bridge for the B&O before his departure from the company. The board, not trusting Long's truss to carry trains, allowed him to erect a single, 107.6-foot, wooden-truss bridge to carry the Washington Road over the main stem's tracks west of Baltimore. Performing well for many years, Long's bridge was an undeniable success and proved the practicality of his truss design. Long's truss, patented in 1830, found acceptance on many other railroads.

Wever's victory meant that between Baltimore and Harpers Ferry the B&O erected masonry viaducts and culverts under his supervision. For many of these he hired his favorite contractor, Robert Wilson. But the departure of the army engineers was only a short-lived victory for the carpenter engineers, as the profession was steadily changing to a scientific basis. Knight's and Wever's appointments simply show the company's reliance and trust in the conventional and familiar type of engineer, instead of the virtually unknown formalized professionalism of Long and McNeill.[7] But as the B&O's new engineers rose through the ranks in the wake of the 1830 disagreements, professionalism and a scientific attention to detail became the norm in the engineering community. Like many other civilian engineers across the country, Benjamin Latrobe Jr. came to respect and emulate the military engineers' use of scientifically based engineering, but he also appreciated the talents of veterans like Wernwag, and the two got along well.

The company continued spending much time and money on masonry structures--with one notable exception. Only two years after dismissing Long's wooden truss as unfit, the railroad was forced by a lack of time and money to build a wooden bridge across the Monocacy River, some 20 miles east of Harpers Ferry.[8] By this time Wernwag must have changed his opinion on wooden railroad bridges, for he built a three-span, 330-foot-long bridge that marked the first use of timber trusses on the main stem. This 1831 bridge was likely the first wooden railroad bridge in America.[9] It was probably a deck truss strengthened with arches (resembling the Burr arch truss in Figure 3) following one of Wernwag's unpatented designs.

On one hand, the success of professional engineers in applying structural theory and mathematics to their wooden-truss designs finally removed the doubts of traditional carpenter-engineers. But most crucial to the acceptance of timber bridges on the B&O (and other lines) was their low cost and rapid construction, when a repeated rebuilding was cheaper than the cost of a masonry viaduct. The B&O, running low on funds by the time it reached Harpers Ferry, had little choice but to build with wood--thereafter adopting wooden bridges with little remorse for the scorn heaped on Colonel Long five years before. Ironically, the Potomac bridge would mark the end of Wever's work for the B&O, and was Wernwag's last major project before his death. Likewise, Knight would afterwards turn many of the chief engineer's responsibilities over to Benjamin Latrobe--the representative of the new order in American civil engineering. Like few other places, Harpers Ferry marks the changeover from the carpenter engineer to the professionally trained engineer, and the acceptance of wooden railroad bridges.

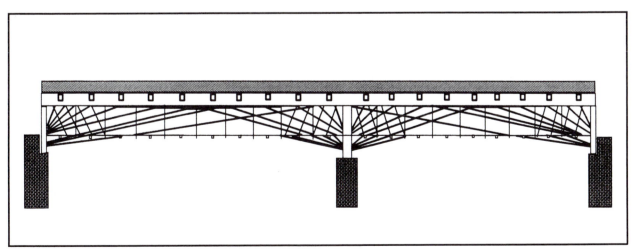

*Figure 5-A schematic of the arch-brace truss layout on the Schauffhausen bridge, built across the Rhine River in Germany during the 1750s. Arch braces had been used for centuries to increase the spans of pile-and-beam bridges and were sometimes used on other truss layouts for added strength, but the Schauffhausen bridge carried their use to a new level. Latrobe modified this system and, beginning with the Harpers Ferry bridge in 1836, used it for the B&O's wooden bridges until ca 1850. (IHTIA, drawing by author.)*

### Latrobe's Bridge Design For Harpers Ferry: The Latrobian Truss

Latrobe's plan to cross the Potomac called for a wooden bridge (with wrought- and cast-iron components) approximately 900 feet long from abutment to abutment. It had seven spans of varying lengths, the longest of which was 135 feet from end to end of the truss (dimensions of the bridge are given in detail in the following section). Each span consisted of three parallel trusses to provide double lanes; the turnpike occupied the upstream side and the railroad the downstream side. The first eastern span crossed the C&O Canal basin angled to the rest of the bridge to ease the line's curvature at the foot of Maryland Heights. The remainder of the bridge sat on a nearly east-west axis.

At Harpers Ferry Latrobe did not use either Wernwag's or Long's truss systems, or any other standard type. Instead, Latrobe oddly found inspiration in a well-known German covered bridge over the Rhine River at Schauffhausen, and mimicked its truss system in the Harpers Ferry crossing. The Schauffhausen bridge was built around 1755 by Swiss carpenter Ulric Grubenmann, and was one of the very first long-span, wooden-truss bridges built in modern times.[10] It consisted of two spans of 172 feet and 193 feet, with a single mid-river pier, and was a curious design called an *arch-brace truss*. The truss system was simplistic, except it incorporated numerous inclined braces extending out from the abutments to points

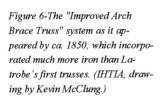

*Figure 6-The "Improved Arch Brace Truss" system as it appeared by ca. 1850, which incorporated much more iron than Latrobe's first trusses. (IHTIA, drawing by Kevin McClung.)*

along the top chord. The result was a combination of overlapping, independently acting segmented arches. Although admirable, the Schauffhausen bridge's truss system had serious faults. In particular, the truss panels lacked sufficient counter-bracing, making it somewhat unstable.[11] Further, unlike most trusses which transferred the load vertically down into the abutments, the arch braces applied a great deal of horizontal thrust to the tops of the abutments, requiring more substantial masonry than other trusses of comparable dimensions.

Latrobe's truss layout for the Harpers Ferry bridge resembled a Howe truss, with verticals in tension and diagonals under compression. But the dominant feature was the Schauffhausen-type arch braces which radiated from the abutment out to a progressively thicker top chord. Only the central panels were left without arch braces to support them. Latrobe attempted to correct the faults of the Schauffhausen bridge (mostly succeeding) by adding a diagonal brace across each panel and two diagonals across each central panel to stiffen the design. Iron was also used, but only sparingly at first. The arch braces were seated in cast-iron shoes, which in turn were seated in cast-iron "skewbacks" or abutment blocks sitting on masonry piers. The lower chord, tying together the skewbacks at each end of the truss, was under tension and countered the outward thrust of the arch braces, similar to a bowstring arch.

This overall configuration has been termed the *Latrobian truss* by historian

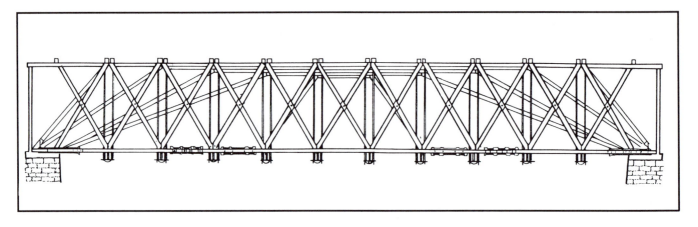

Robert Vogel. Exactly why Latrobe favored this relatively obscure truss system while others would have served equally well is unclear, but he may have wanted to escape patent licensing fees, saving the railroad much-needed funds. Vogel suggests an alternative:

> It is quite likely that Latrobe did not have absolute confidence in the various pure truss systems already patented by Town, Long, and others, and preferred for such strategic service a structure in which the panel members acted more or less independently of one another.[12]

After gaining experience with his truss system, Latrobe began revising the design, incorporating two diagonals in every panel for counterbracing to further stiffen the bridge.[13] Latrobe also encountered a common problem in wooden trusses--that the weakest points were tension member joints. Latrobe and other engineers dealt with this by beginning to use wrought-iron rods for tension members in lieu of timber. This was first officially done with the Howe truss, patented in 1840. Continually improving his design, Latrobe replaced the vertical, wooden tension members with adjustable wrought-iron rods connected to cast-iron bearing plates. Such wrought-iron rods were easily "retrofitted" to an older bridge, and the later modifications of the Latrobian design were incorporated in the Harpers Ferry bridge. So, while the Latrobian truss was originally almost all wooden, iron became an integral part of the design--probably in the early 1840s. There were larger, adjustable, cast-iron skewbacks, and cast and wrought-iron turnbuckles spliced together the timbers making up the bottom chord, allowing the bottom chord to be adjusted to the engineer's wishes and kept under tension.

Cast iron, although cheaper than wrought iron, was often of low (or unknown) quality at the time and useful only for such fixtures as "shoes" for the timber beams, or bearing plates between joints. This was primarily because iron shops could not control the quality of their large

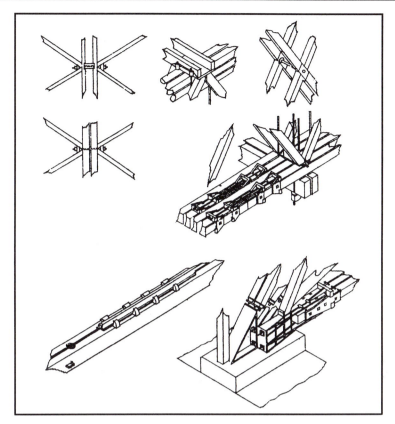

castings, which were often invisibly flawed. Conversely, wrought iron was of generally high quality, possessing greater resistance to tensile forces. Yet, because of its high cost and unavailability in large structural members, wrought iron was used only for tension rods to strengthen timber trusses. Wood, like cast iron, performed better as a compression member. Only when reliable cast iron could be produced consistently in large quantities would it fully take the place of wood for compression members and true all-iron trusses come into use.

By 1850, a Latrobian truss bridge 145 feet long incorporated 63,000 board feet of lumber, 57,156 pounds of cast iron, and 15,340 pounds of wrought iron.[14] The arch-brace truss was the standard B&O bridge until about 1850. Herman Haupt, another great nineteenth-century bridge engineer, said in 1851 of the Latrobian truss:

> It is an admirable combination, possessing every essential of a well-proportioned and scientifically arranged structure. It is a system of counter-braces and

*Figure 7-Details of Latrobe's improved truss, ca. 1850, showing the blending of wood, cast iron, and wrought iron. Clockwise from bottom right: the cast-iron skewback and adjustable connection to the bottom chord; the attachment of rails to stringers; adjustable transverse brace connections (with wrought-iron rods) for both the bottom and top chord; the intersection of an upper transverse strut with the top chord; the connection between diagonals; and the intersection of a transverse floor beam and bottom chord showing a bottom chord splice--note the wrought-iron suspension rods. (From Haupt, **General Theory of Bridge Construction**, Plate 12.)*

braces. In its general principle it bears some resemblance to the celebrated bridge across the Rhine at Schauffhausen, but the latter, owing to the absence of counter-braces, was so flexible that it would vibrate with the weight of a single man, whilst the Baltimore and Ohio R.R. Bridge is so rigid that the heaviest locomotives, running with great velocity, produce but very little effect.[15]

Though praised by many and successful on the B&O for about twenty years, Latrobe's improved truss was not perfect. Vogel makes the point that, "They were...more empirical than efficient and were, for the most part, not only grossly overdesigned but of decidedly difficult fabrication and construction."[16]

While the credit for designing the Harpers Ferry bridge usually goes to Latrobe, and the truss design now bears his name, he must have relied heavily on the expertise of Lewis Wernwag. Latrobe had yet to build a wooden bridge when given the job of designing the Potomac crossing, and it is hard to imagine him not looking to the veteran bridge builder for guidance. Latrobe and the aging Wernwag met at Harpers Ferry in the fall of 1835, and the two struck up a friendship. Bad weather prevented the two from working one day, and they spent time in Wernwag's machine shop on Virginius Island looking at structural models. "Wernwag is certainly a most uncommon man," Latrobe commented in his journal. "His conceptions of complicated machinery are exceedingly clear and ingenious. He is a thoroughbred German in his dialect & manners and knew my father 35 years ago."[17] Wernwag's German origins probably made him aware of the Schauffhausen bridge, and he may have suggested that Latrobe use its basic form. After meeting Wernwag, Latrobe predicted, "It seems destined that I should deal in all sorts of bridges."[18] Wernwag's pioneering use of iron in earlier trusses suggests his input on the Harpers Ferry design as well. There is no question, however, that the B&O's first Potomac bridge at Harpers Ferry repre-sents the work of both great engineers, and is an excellent example of the transitional period between all-wood and all-iron bridges.

## Notes

1. Letter, Lewis Wernwag to Philip Thomas, 1829. Originally included in Long, Stephen H., *Description of the Jackson Bridge*, Baltimore, 1830.

2. Calhoun, *The American Civil Engineer, Origins and Conflict*, 120-133.

3. Smith, *The Book of the Great Railway Celebrations of 1857*, 12-13.

4. Calhoun, 123.

5. Ibid., 126.

6. Letter, Lewis Wernwag to Philip Thomas, 1829.

7. Calhoun, 128-129.

8. *Baltimore and Ohio Railroad Sixth Annual Report*, 1831, 106.

9. Condit, *American Building Art: The Nineteenth Century*, 88.

10. Kirby, *The Early Years of Modern Civil Engineering*, 140.

11. Haupt, *General Theory of Bridge Construction*, 145.

12. Vogel, "The Engineering Contributions of Wendel Bollman," 85.

13. Haupt, 146.

14. Ibid., 254.

15. Ibid., 253.

16. Vogel, 85.

17. As quoted in Dilts, *The Great Road*, 206, from the B.H. Latrobe Jr., Journal, MS Gamble Collection, Maryland Historical Society.

18. Ibid., 206.

# PART THREE:

# The Evolution of the B&O Railroad at Harpers Ferry and Links to Broader Trends in American Bridge Engineering from 1836 to 1858

## Abutment and Pier Construction, 1835-1836

With Latrobe's design for the bridge superstructure nearing completion, the B&O was ready to begin construction of the abutments and piers. On September 10, 1835, an announcement appeared in the *Virginia Free Press,* giving a detailed description of the required masonry work.

> Proposals will be received by the subscriber at Harpers Ferry, on Saturday the 19th of this month, for the construction of the Masonry of the Viaduct, to be built across the Potomac River at that place. The masonry will consist of one abutment and seven piers. [The Winchester & Potomac was responsible for building the west abutment, and there were six piers, not seven.] The face of the abutments and piers will be of ranged rustic masonry extending inwards an average of at least two feet from the exterior - the filling of six of the piers and the backing of the abutments to be of the best rubble masonry, and the whole laid in the best mortar. The foundations of six of the piers will be formed in the bed of the river by throwing in large stones and compactly fitting the interstices between them with smaller stone. The foundation will be raised from the bottom of the river to within two feet of the surface of low water, at which level the ranged work will commence. One of the piers will stand upon the tow path of the Chesapeake and Ohio Canal, will be built hollow and filled with dry rubble stone and earth. The foundation of this pier will be of ranged work laid in water cement, and the lower course will rest on puddling clay about two feet in depth. The thickness of the walls of the solid part of this pier will be six feet. The six piers in the river will be ten feet thick at bottom and eight feet at top, twenty-five feet high and fifty feet long, with their ends, both up and down stream, of a curved form, resembling the gothic arch. The Abutments will be built against and united to the wall between the canal and the rail road. It is believed that the water, in which the piers will be founded, will in no case exceed seven feet in depth at the low stage of the river, and for most of the piers will not be more than four to five feet deep; and that the bed of the river at the site of the bridge, is entirely of rock.[2]

By mutual agreement between the B&O and the W&P, the W&P funded construction on the west abutment--the contracting firm of Lamb & Lukens got the job--while the B&O funded the east abutment and river piers. Charles Wilson received the B&O's contract for the piers and east abutment.[3] Construction began in the fall of 1835, and workers built earthen cofferdams in the river at the site of each pier. By this time Latrobe had gone off to work temporarily on the Baltimore & Port Deposit Railroad, and was not in charge of construction at Harpers Ferry. The B&O's construction supervisor for the piers was Casper Wever, while Wernwag only concerned himself with preparation of the superstructure. Wever, commenting on Wilson and Wernwag, reported "both...are well known to the Company as contractors of skill, energy and fidelity...."[4]

The west abutment was located on the riverbank downstream from Wager's bridge, and formed the point between the Potomac and Shenandoah Rivers. There were six piers altogether; five piers sat in mid-river, designated here from west to east as piers A, B, C, D, and E.[5] The upstream end of each river pier was pointed to lessen the impact of water and debris, while the downstream end was rounded. Pier F was trapezoidal in plan and built into the towpath. This towpath pier was larger because the "canal span," a funnel-shaped skewed truss, sat angled to the rest of the bridge and required a wider pier. The east abutment was built into the inner retaining wall supporting the railroad along the C&O Canal.

The abutments and piers were built with Tomstown Formation limestone, exhibiting pitch-faced coursed ashlar masonry.[6] The piers' coursed-rubble cores were Harpers Formation phyllite laid in mortar. Some individual rubble slabs were keyed into the limestone facing blocks and extended across the interior of the piers for added strength.[7]

Latrobe, during his time with the B&PD, visited Harpers Ferry and noticed the river piers were not being built to his plan. The abutments on either bank were

*Figure 1-A plan view of the B&O's bridge as it existed from 1836 to 1840. Wager's bridge, just upstream, was taken out of service and demolished in 1838. (IHTIA, drawing by Kevin McClung.)*

*Figure 2-A schematic of the 1836 bridge without its wooden cover, revealing the underlying Latrobian truss. Not to scale. (IHTIA, drawing by author.)*

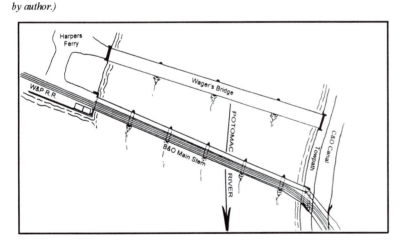

of substantial construction and reflected Latrobe's design, but the masonry in the river piers, particularly that of the foundations, was undersized and of poor quality. "The work is rough and the design not adhered to in the forms of the piers. It will be strong however. Wernwag is preparing for the superstructure, which he will frame at Wever's Mill, 3 miles below the scite.[sic]"[8] Wever's incorporation of undersized masonry would prove disastrous.

## Erecting the Superstructure

The stone piers were finished in mid-1836, and Wernwag began erection of the superstructure that fall.[9] Once the timber for the spans was properly shaped and test assembled to ensure everything fit together, Wernwag built falsework in the river upon which he and his crews erected the various truss members.

When Latrobe returned full-time to the B&O in August of 1836, Chief Engineer Knight appointed him Engineer of Location and Construction, which also made him superintendent of the Potomac bridge. Upon inspecting the bridge with some of the B&O's directors in August of 1836, he could not have been happy. Wernwag had completed the first of the trusses, and Latrobe commented, "It is a beautiful combination of timbers, but the lumber of which it is built is rough stuff."[10] A drought had idled water-powered sawmills the previous year, and there was a shortage of quality lumber in the region. The lumber used in the bridge would cause problems for its entire existence.

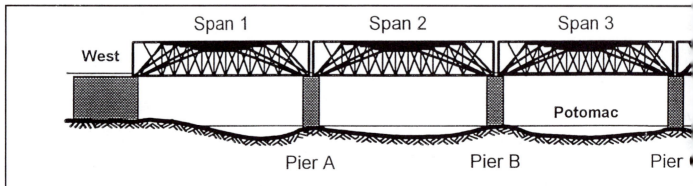

In October of 1836, Latrobe reported that the "viaduct" at Harpers Ferry was nearly finished.[11] That month, a blacksmith named Odey was "putting some irons to the timbers" of the bridge, when he fell into the river and drowned, the only known death to occur during construction.[12] Workers finally completed the trusses in December of 1836, and a single track of iron u-shaped rails was laid across the new structure. Wernwag removed the falsework and the bridge stood on its own. The bridge opened to rail and turnpike traffic in January 1837--with the press announcing that "locomotives and their trains have passed over it."[13] The locomotive was a temporary luxury, and horses hauled freight over the bridge and through the narrows for another year, until the canal company relented on the requirement and allowed locomotives to pass. For the time being the trusses remained uncovered, exposing them to the elements.

*Figure 4-A drawing of Harpers Ferry, ca. 1837, showing the B&O's new bridge (in the background) and Wager's bridge. (Hahn Collection.)*

| Span Number/ Other Name | Clear Span | Truss Length |
|---|---|---|
| 7/Canal span | 122' | App. 130' |
| 6 | 76' | 85' |
| 5 | 126' 9" | 134' 5" |
| 4 | 127' | 135' |
| 3 | 126' 6" | 134' 5" |
| 2 | 126' 6" | 134' |
| 1/Winchester span | 124' | 127' 6" |

*Figure 3-Details (from east to west) of the 1836 bridge. Its overall length was approximately 875 feet. The depth (or height) of each truss was about 15 feet. (Measurements from the **Baltimore and Ohio Railroad Thirty-Second Annual Report, 1858.**)*

There was trouble with the bridge, however, and scandal reared its head. After receiving reports that something was wrong with the bridge, Latrobe discovered the trusses were unstable under load. Examining the mid-river piers, Latrobe found the masonry cracking under the weight of the timber superstructure--the product of Wever's too-light stonework. The river had also scoured under some of the piers, and Latrobe realized the foundations had not been carried down to solid rock. The abutments on either side of the river were safe, but the deterioration of the river piers brought on the very real possibility that the bridge might soon collapse.

Latrobe quickly formulated a plan suggesting the piers should be wrapped with iron bands and stabilized. Instead, the board of directors stalled, and in March of 1837 appointed Latrobe, Jonathan Knight, and Charles Fisk (the canal company engineer) to investigate the causes and possi-

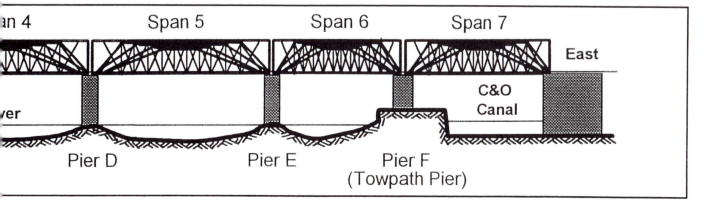

ble solutions for the poor masonry in lieu of immediate repairs. By the time they presented their findings (some two months later) the piers had degraded to the point that stabilization was no longer possible and some piers needed major repairs. It was an embarrassing situation for the company.

An official company inquiry found that Wever and the private contractor, Charles Wilson, were both to blame for the bad stonework and shallow foundations. They were also guilty of some rather suspicious business practices--a charge Wever had faced before. Wever had chosen the highest bidder on the contract, Wilson, who in turn purchased the stone for the piers from one of Wever's own private quarries. Unlike the better stone from local quarries which went into the abutments, the stone from Wever's quarry, which was 3 miles away, was of poorer quality. It was also more expensive and the railroad was obligated to haul it to the bridge site. Then, just before construction started, Wever quietly made changes in Latrobe's plan for the piers, substituting a design with smaller foundations and smaller masonry blocks--like those produced at his quarry. The board of directors, trusting Wever, approved his changes to the plan without question. He was then sent off on route surveys west of Harpers Ferry. Wilson, the contractor, laid the masonry according to the altered plans with little supervision from other company officials. What happened was probably criminal, but no charges were ever brought, and the company never proved collusion between Wilson and Wever.[14]

Wever retired from the company on the day Latrobe returned to work for the railroad, marking the end to an intriguing chapter in the B&O's engineering department. The debacle at Harpers Ferry was Wever's last, and probably most blatant, of a long line of such activities dating back six years to the great debate with Col. Long. The company had not heeded Long's warnings concerning Wever's questionable dealings, and for Wever, his activities at Harpers Ferry had been busi-

ness as usual. Latrobe would thereafter operate the engineering department in the style Long had lobbied for. Thus, the Harpers Ferry bridge represented the final battle within the B&O between these two opposing eras of American civil engineering.

## Repair of the Bridge Piers and Superstructure

The Wever-induced failure became Latrobe's problem. To make matters worse, three transverse floor beams on the bridge cracked without warning during the passage of a train in September 1837. Latrobe soon formulated a plan that would save the great bridge and reinforce the superstructure as well. The company contracted with Lewis Wernwag to erect trestlework, raise the bridge off its piers, and repair the superstructure. William Lester received the contract to repair the piers. The pier foundations were rebuilt, and stone rip-rap laid in a fish-scale pattern around the base of each for erosion protection. Approximately 5 feet of stonework was rebuilt at the top of each pier. This allowed Latrobe to add ornate, semi-circular coping stones to the downstream end of each pier. Latrobe recounted the year's work at Harpers Ferry in an October 1837 stockholders' report. He wrote:

> The third work carried on under my supervision, has been the completion and repair of the Harper's Ferry Viaduct, and some walling and rail laying appurtenant thereto....Both these parts of the work were proceeding with satisfactory speed; the trussels [sic] were framed ready for use, the foundation masonry was well advanced, and the dressed stone for the repairs of the piers was in process of speedy preparation. The viaduct in the mean time, however, appearing to endure with less apparent injury than had been looked for, the action of the travel upon it, which had never been suspended, though cautiously conducted, and the season having arrived during which freshets in the rivers at the immediate confluence of which the bridge was situated, might be expected, and the occurrence of which would have endangered the superstructure while depending on the trussels for support---the board, at

their meeting on October 4th, determined to postpone until the ensuing spring the proposed repairs of the upper parts of the defective piers, proceeding, however with the stone work for the security of their foundations, which work was completed about the middle of this month, in the most satisfactory manner, and places the foundations of the piers, it is believed, beyond the reach of future injury by the operations of the currents of the rivers.[15]

Latrobe then discussed the ominous cracking of three transverse floor beams and their subsequent reinforcing. He defended the principle of the arch-brace truss, but his praise for the superstructure was somewhat overblown considering the rough timbering and its tendency to fracture.

> The wooden superstructure of the bridge has justified the confidence entertained, in the excellence of its principle of construction.... The recurrence of such a fracture, caused by an accidental imperfection in one the of the timbers which failed, will be effectually prevented by the proposed immediate introduction of an additional timber between each of those upon which the floor and tracks depend for their support.[16]

While the bridge was repaired, carpenters weatherboarded and roofed the C&O Canal span. The other trusses would remain uncovered through much of the winter. One of the carpenters working on the bridge was Wendel Bollman, just re-hired by the company and soon to be made foreman of bridges (Bollman is discussed in detail later). While the bridge's total cost is not known, the company spent $23,450.60 to complete it during 1837, and $5,596.34 on subsequent repairs that year alone.[17] Latrobe's problems were not over, and another floor beam cracked in the spring of the next year. That year the B&O spent an additional $7,270.75 on repairs to the bridge.[18] During its first six years, the bridge was constantly under repair. It required, in fact, some sort of upkeep or reconstruction nearly every year of its life.

*Figure 5-Latrobe's 1837 repairs to the piers are visible in this closeup of a ca. 1859 photo. (NPS photo.)*

The new bridge became the primary highway crossing of the Potomac River in the vicinity of Harpers Ferry. An act of the Virginia General Assembly transferred the turnpike traffic from Wager's bridge to the new B&O bridge, although Wager continued to collect the same foot and wagon traffic tolls.[19] At first there was a small walkway along the Potomac bridge's downstream side for tow animals to pull barges from the Shenandoah River Lock, across to the river lock on the C&O Canal. It was removed in 1841.[20] A small, wooden stairway on the upstream side of the towpath pier gave teamsters, boat operators, and travellers access to the bridge and C&O Canal towpath. Crossing gates controlled turnpike access at each end of the bridge, and stopped traffic as trains approached. It was the only bridge on the line which required such gates, necessitated by the heavy turnpike traffic and the mid-river grade crossing. A bridge watchman permanently guarded against fires, while also operating the gates upon the approach of trains.[21]

When Latrobe originally designed his bridge, his primary desire was to align directly with the W&P's grade. The B&O otherwise had no definite plans upon reaching Harpers Ferry, and there were serious questions whether the main stem would continue from there. Ultimately, once the B&O decided to continue west the Potomac bridge's alignment was quite unsatisfactory.

### The B&O's First Harpers Ferry Depot

Just prior to the completion of the bridge, the B&O's president predicted that once it was open, "The passenger and burden trains of the two companies will then stop, side by side, in the same depot, and the transit from one to the other will be effected promptly and with great convenience."[22] In 1836 the company purchased a lot in lower Harpers Ferry at the west end of the new bridge, south of the W&P's tracks, and built a small ticket office in late 1836 or early 1837.[23] However, freight interchange here was problematic, and Harpers Ferry lacked adequate freight facilities for many years. Much of the freight to be loaded or unloaded sat in boxcars on a siding along the north shore of the Potomac directly across from town.

### A Summary of the B&O's Situation in 1838

For a short while Harpers Ferry was the western terminus of the B&O. Upon reaching Harpers Ferry, work on extending the railroad further toward the Ohio stalled while the B&O searched for funds, legal permission, and leadership; most importantly, the railroad needed an acceptable route. Although the company had (nearly) always considered Cumberland as a logical goal in its quest for the Ohio River, in light of the canal compromise the railroad's exact route west from Harpers Ferry was not immediately clear. Additional surveys through Maryland and Virginia toward the summits of the Alleghenies were needed, some of which proposed bypassing Harpers Ferry altogether. Worse, the line between Baltimore and Harpers Ferry already needed extensive repair and upgrades to incorporate the lessons learned by engineers in the preceding decade. By 1838, the B&O was ready to continue west using a more modern building style. The company had learned important lessons in reaching Harpers Ferry.

The B&O considered the pause here temporary. Its leaders well understood the need to press on to the Ohio to fulfill the railroad's potential and justify the cost of construction. After completion of the Potomac bridge in 1836, the B&O's president commented:

> There is hardly a rail road in the country, that has been completed, that is not now realizing a handsome return on the cost of its construction: and the chief reason why this is not done by the Baltimore and Ohio Rail Road, is, that it is not completed. If it were, at this day, proposed to make a rail road to Fredericktown [sic] or Harpers' Ferry-(supposing the Baltimore and Ohio Railroad to the west not to be projected even,) no one would be willing to undertake such a work through so difficult a region....[24]

In the meantime, the B&O's freight and passenger traffic increased dramatically after its arrival in Harpers Ferry. As hoped, the Winchester and Potomac supplied large amounts of freight and passengers from the Shenandoah Valley. Turnpike stagecoaches also met the B&O here at its temporary western terminus, conveying freight and passengers across the mountains on the National Road to the Ohio River at Wheeling.

### The Main Stem Continues West from Harpers Ferry

As a result of the canal agreement and delays in acquiring an extended charter from the Virginia legislature, the B&O had ample time to study the issue of a route west of Harpers Ferry. As chief engineer, Jonathan Knight carried out many of the preliminary route surveys through the Potomac Valley, but Benjamin Latrobe Jr. was in charge of most location and design work on the B&O main stem after 1836. They focused on the region west and north of Harpers Ferry, searching for a route to Cumberland, and then over the summit of the Alleghenies and on to Wheeling and/or Pittsburgh.[25] In October of 1836 Latrobe summed up the goals of the previous summer's surveys with astute clarity, illustrating the main issues facing the company's engineers:

The route through its entire length, presented many interesting questions with respect to its location, but the points of peculiar and pressing importance were two:

First--The crossing of the Alleghany range of mountains, from the eastern to the western waters.

Second--The ascent of the valley of the Potomac, from Harpers Ferry or its vicinity, to the eastern base of those mountains at the town of Cumberland. The difficulties to be surmounted in the accomplishment of the former object were altogether of a physical description, dependent upon the bold features of the alpine region through which a passage was to be effected; while the latter, principally grew out of the preoccupation of the Maryland side of the valley by the Chesapeake and Ohio canal.[26]

The Potomac Valley presented the most logical route for reaching Cumberland, which the B&O considered second in importance only to reaching the Ohio River.[27] Yet the C&O Canal's occupation of the north bank to Cumberland, combined with a lack of space on the south bank, brought up numerous conflicts with the canal's route that required multiple crossings of the Potomac, each promising delays and high costs. This made construction though the Potomac Valley for at least 30 miles upstream from Harpers Ferry out of the question.[28] The Baltimore and Ohio's viable options consisted of a variety of routes, although all followed essentially two different, broad, corridors--one crossing through Maryland, the other through Virginia. The Maryland routes departed from the main stem east of Harpers Ferry and passed northward through Hagerstown. The Virginia corridor continued from Harpers Ferry and stayed south of the Potomac most of the distance to Cumberland, eliminating the problems presented by the canal.

The latter required the line to leave the main valley of the Potomac and cut across the interior of Jefferson and Berkeley counties, outflanking numerous narrows and large bends in the river and returning to the Potomac's south shore

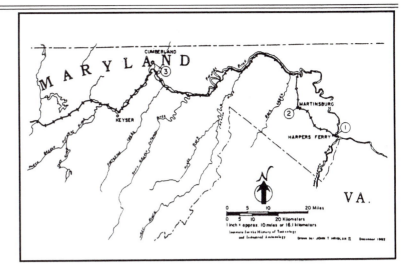

*Figure 6-The B&O's route in the Potomac Valley west of Harpers Ferry showing (1) Harpers Ferry, (2) Martinsburg, and (3) Cumberland. (IHTIA, drawing by John Hriblan.)*

nearly 40 miles upstream from Harpers Ferry. But the presence of the federal armory in lower Harpers Ferry seemingly blocked any use of the Potomac's south shore upstream of town. Additionally, the Potomac bridge's orientation toward the W&P's line made the engineers look first to the Shenandoah Valley for an escape route. By leasing 6 miles of the Winchester and Potomac's line south from Harpers Ferry, the B&O could leave the Shenandoah Valley near Charlestown before turning back to the northwest, passing through Martinsburg, and returning to the Potomac. By the end of 1837 the surveys had demonstrated the feasibility of this route, and the B&O entered negotiations with the Winchester & Potomac. These negotiations would prove fruitless.

Meanwhile, Latrobe's surveying crews had discovered a route out of the Potomac Valley just upstream from Harpers Ferry--if a right-of-way through the armory grounds could be acquired. This route left the Potomac Valley along Elk Run 1.5 miles above town and linked with the previously surveyed route across Jefferson and Berkeley counties. In particular, the party under assistant engineer H.R. Hazelhurst followed, "A route on the Virginia side of the Potomac, from Harper's Ferry to that river at the North mountain, and which is traced by the ravines of Elk run, Tuscarora creek and Talasses branch, and by the town of Martinsburgh [sic]...."[29] This was the route the company eventually settled upon, but only after negotiating the armory right-of-way.

The federal armory occupied all the level ground along the Potomac River, and the Secretary of War was initially hesitant to allow the railroad access, but the parties finally reached an agreement in mid-1838.[30] It required the B&O to build a lengthy trestle atop a parallel set of walls along the armory, helping protect it from floodwaters. But now the B&O's bridge was pointing up the wrong river and something would have to be done.

Once the armory issue was settled, Virginia legislators finalized the B&O's route from Harpers Ferry in November 1838. The B&O's new president, Louis McLane, led the effort to acquire the new charter, as well as partial funding for the line, from the state of Virginia. The new charter specifically required the main stem to cross into Virginia at Harpers Ferry, then continue only in Virginia to a point some 5 miles below Cumberland, where the line could cross the Potomac River back into Maryland. It also stipulated that Wheeling, Virginia, must be made one of the termini for the completed line.[31] Though seemingly restrictive, it was largely dictated by the B&O's wishes and appeared to be the shortest (98 miles) and cheapest route. The legislature allowed construction for another five years from 1838.

The B&O's route to Cumberland passed through only one town of any size, Martinsburg, while the rest of the way the B&O traversed long distances of sparsely populated river valley. Only Cumberland held out the prospect of revenues from passengers and freight needed to pay off past loans and continue construction. However, the B&O's earlier agreement that the C&O Canal must reach Cumberland before the railroad still prevented construction. The canal had advanced only half the distance in the preceeding five years and, under pressure from both Virginia and Maryland, it relented in its competition with the railroad and agreed to let the B&O begin building anew.

*Figure 7-A plan view of the Latrobe/Wernwag bridge after the 1842 reconstruction to turn the main stem up the Potomac. (IHTIA, drawing by Kevin McClung.)*

America's financial panic of 1837 nearly brought work to a halt just as it got underway (progress stalled on many other internal improvements elsewhere in the country), but the B&O managed to continue. For Harpers Ferry, renewal of the main stem's construction from there ensured its importance as a stopping point and branch-line junction. After renewal of the charter in 1838, the board of directors directed Latrobe to prepare the route to Cumberland and advertise for contractors.[32] Construction began along a section near Martinsburg, 20 miles west of Harpers Ferry, in August of the following year.[33] At Harpers Ferry, the contracts awaited Latrobe's decision on how to turn the tracks onto the armory grounds. During 1839 the B&O purchased the remaining toll and ferry rights along the Potomac's south shore and finally dismantled Wager's bridge.[34] Construction was particularly intense at Harpers Ferry; the company simultaneously reconfigured the Potomac bridge, built an extensive river wall and trestle, erected three other new bridges, and dug a tunnel.

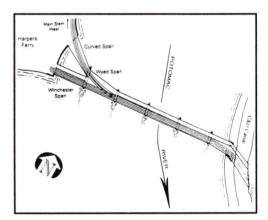

## 1840-1842 Bridge Reconstruction

The requirement to turn the main stem up the Potomac on the armory walls, then just being built, presented a perplexing problem for Latrobe. There was no room in lower Harpers Ferry to form a junction with the W&P and still make an acceptable turn onto the armory wall. In order to get the main stem's track turned 90 degrees toward the armory wall, La-

trobe rebuilt the west end of the bridge into a "Y". The western most river pier (pier A) was extended upstream 38 feet, giving it an overall length of 90 feet. Workers removed most of the center-line truss on span number two and angled the upstream truss toward the new armory wall, making the span funnel-shaped. The lack of a true center truss opened up the interior of span number two, and it became a crossroads. Here Latrobe created a junction with the W&P that resembled a track wye (shaped like a Y). Span two became known as the "wyed span." This was also written as "wide span" since it was wider than the others, and "Y'd" span. The existing Harpers Ferry to Frederick Turnpike was now forced to cross over the B&O's tracks on the wyed span immediately west of the W&P's junction.

To carry the sharply curving main stem from pier A to the shore, Latrobe added a completely new span number one (from this point on the original span number one is referred to solely as the Winchester span). Span one, which became known as the "curved span," was funnel-shaped to allow for the curvature started on span two. Span number one's western end rested on a newly built abutment, which had a wingwall/causeway, approximately 25 feet high and 25 feet wide, extending upstream about 250 feet. The wingwall supported the tracks *and* acted as an abutment for a short span crossing the "boatway" onto the armory walls. The boatway gap--between the wingwall/causeway and the armory walls--provided access to the old ferry landing and the river. The new abutment and wingwall incorporated parts of the old abutment from the recently demolished Wager bridge. The rail-

| Span Number/Other Name | Clear Span | Truss Length |
|---|---|---|
| #1/Curved span | 130' 6" | 138' |
| #2/Wyed span | 126' 6" | 134' |

road acquired property in the lower town for their new right-of-way between the bridge and the armory, and in February of 1840 construction began.

The company completed the bridge reconstruction by 1842 and reinforced the trusses of the remaining spans. In many ways it was a completely new bridge. Yet, the mid-river junction with the W&P and the turnpike crossing, both within the confines of the wyed span, was decidedly inconvenient. It was certainly a gamble on Latrobe's part. Although he made the best of a bad situation, the wyed span infringed on efficient train operations for the remainder of its history. It was a spectacular structure, however, and dominated the scene with its odd shape. William Prescott Smith later described it as "remarkable not so much for its length as for its peculiar form, the ends being curved in opposite directions, and the structure bifurcated towards the western extremity."[35] Subsequent bridges built at the

crossing would follow the same layout for nearly sixty years.

## Architectural Adornment

The company had completely covered the sides of the bridge with horizontal clapboards, and applied a metal roof during its first years. This covering was removed during reconstruction, and not replaced until at least mid-1841.[36] After the creation of the wyed span, Latrobe adorned the bridge with imposing architectural details which, in conjunction with the roofline, visually separated the bridge into four distinct parts: the angled canal span, the four river spans, the oversized wyed and curved spans, and the Winchester span. Indeed, the wyed and curved spans took on some particularly intriguing artistic details not usually found on covered bridges. Vertical post moldings, resembling doric columns, stood out from the clapboard. Unlike the simple, unadorned pitched roof of the rest of the bridge, these two spans were topped by an

*Figure 10-The curved span's portal, added during the 1842 reconstruction. Note the architectural details on the wyed and curved spans. This view from atop the trestle also shows the passenger platform at right, and the facades of the Potomac Restaurant and Wager House Hotel. Photo ca. 1859. (West Virginia and Regional History Collection.)*

ornate cornice, supported by posts extending above the column moldings, and braces reaching out from the roof to the facade at each post. The posts supported the cornice some 5 feet above the sidewalls, with rectangular openings piercing the cornice between the columns. These rectangular openings, while aesthetically appealing and adding lightness to the wyed span's appearance, probably served the purpose of allowing rainwater and snow to run off the roof.

The west end of the bridge (the curved span) incorporated an oversized, ornate portal, with inclined columns of a somewhat bizarre, neo-Egyptian style. At least two other covered bridges on the line west of Harpers Ferry had similar portals. The canal span's eastern portal was not quite so large and the columns were not inclined. A cornice also protruded above the roof line where the canal span and span six met.

## The Armory River Wall, Armory Trestle, and the Government Power Canal Bridge

Crossing the armory grounds proved quite an obstacle, and the B&O let this section out for contract last. The solution for carrying the tracks across the armory grounds was ingenious and another daring move by Latrobe. At that time the government was building a retaining wall 40 feet behind the row of armory shops lining the Potomac River. Latrobe successfully lobbied the federal government to build a parallel wall 20 feet closer to the river, which, in combination with the armory wall, would support a trestle. The agreement stated:

> The outside of this [armory] wall is about forty feet from the river front of said workshops and its top will when finished be about fourteen or fifteen feet above low water in the river the space between the

wall and the shops being filled up and graded as a street. The route for the railroad having reached the United States property at the lower or eastern end of the wall just mentioned, passes up the river on the outside of that wall with a view to the construction of an additional wall in the river parallel to the United States wall and about twenty feet therefrom: this additional wall to be built by the company of such a height as may be deemed necessary to guard against danger from high water to the superstructure that may be placed upon the wall: the United States wall being also raised by the company to such a height as may be deemed necessary for the same purpose: the part so raised not extending inward from the outer face of the wall at its top more than five feet: The space between the two walls to be left open throughout for the passage of the water of the river....[37]

Contracts for the walls and the trestle were let at the end of 1839, with the *Virginia Free Press* announcing:

> Sealed proposals will be received until December 14, for the work to be done upon the 1st section, 1st Residence, 1st Division, Baltimore and Ohio Railroad, west of Harpers Ferry. The section is something more than 1-1/2 miles in length and extends from the Railroad viaduct at Harpers Ferry, upwards along the Virginia shore of the Potomac to a point a little

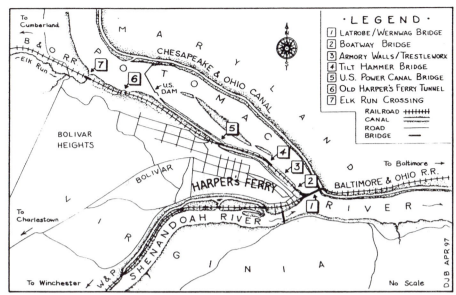

*Figure 11-A map locating major engineering features along the main stem at Harpers Ferry after the line continued west in 1842. (IHTIA, drawing by Daniel Bonenberger.)*

*Figure 12-A ca. 1880 view-from the Maryland shore, showing the engineering features constructed in 1841-42 just upstream of the B&O's bridge. From left to right are: the wing-wall/causeway, the boat-way, and the river wall supporting the armory trestle. (NPS photo.)*

above the Government dam. The work embraces a considerable amount of bridge masonry and wooden superstructure tres-tle work, dry walling, excavation and em-bankment.[38]

Construction began on the new abut-ment, river wall, and the requisite backfill-ing along the armory grounds in February 1840. The B&O's river wall began just af-ter the boatway, and continued at a height of approximately 15 feet above the low water mark for nearly a quarter-mile. There, the refinery forge at the armory used a great waterwheel-powered trip ham-mer, or "tilt hammer," which necessitated a large gap in the wall for a tail race. Passing the tilt hammer gap, the wall con-tinued approximately 120 feet. The river wall was massive, with the top averaging 4.5 feet wide. Numerous small openings, as well as a few larger arched openings, al-lowed water to drain through the walls.

The two walls were a base for a 1,931-foot-long wooden trestle, approximately 10 feet tall, carrying two tracks.[39] The river-side leg of each bent rested on top of the B&O's wall, while each armory-side leg sat on a stone pedestal set onto the in-terior armory wall. Wooden decking on the trestle allowed passengers and crew-men to walk safely, and handrails ran the entire length of either side. The agree-

ment with the government described the proposed trestle:

> The superstructures for the support of the railway upon the parallel walls above de-scribed on route A to consist of wooden tressels [sic] or pillars of brick, stone, or iron, as the company may prefer: the posts of pillars to be placed at least fifteen feet apart from the centre to centre lengthwise of the road, and to be not more than eight-een inches in diameter: the supports to stand in two parallel lines one upon the Government wall raised as above men-tioned and the other upon the parallel wall built by the railroad company....[40]

The company incorporated two short bridges into the trestle to span the gaps in the river wall. The "boatway bridge" was a wooden deck truss consisting of one 31-foot-long span. The span's south end rested on the wingwall/causeway of the Potomac bridge's abutment, while the north end connected to the trestlework on the armory grounds. Approximately 1600 feet upstream of the boatway bridge, the trestle incorporated the "tilt hammer bridge," a deck truss consisting of four 40-foot-long spans.[41]

*Figure 13-A ca. 1859 photo from atop the armory trestle, looking up the Potomac. This is the opposite view from Figure 10. (West Virginia and Regional History Collec-tion.)*

| Trestlework or Bridge Name | Span Length | Number of Spans | Material |
|---|---|---|---|
| Harpers Ferry trestle | 15' | 16 | Wood |
| Boatway bridge | 31' | 1 | Wood |
| Trestlework west | 15' | 92 | Wood |
| Tilt Hammer bridge | 40' | 4 | Wood |
| Government trestle | 10' | 12 | Wood |
| Power canal bridge | 150' | 1 | Wood |

*Figure 14-Details on the trestlework and contiguous bridges, from east to west. The first 16 trestle bents sat on the wingwall/causeway, the next 92 on the armory river walls. In the 1850s this trestle was replaced with an iron version which maintained these span lengths. (Measurements from the Baltimore and Ohio Railroad Thirty-Second Annual Report, 1858.)*

After passing the armory grounds and the last of the trestlework, the line continued along the sliver of land separating the river and the armory power canal. One last bridge would take the line across the Potomac. In 1841 the B&O erected the "power canal bridge"--a wooden, covered bridge consisting of one 148-foot-long span (incorporating Latrobe's arch-brace truss system) resting on granite abutments.[42] Here again Latrobe added ornate portals. In effect, there was now a continuous bridge or trestle, of one sort or another, from the bottom of Maryland Heights to the west end of the power canal bridge--a distance of approximately 4,000 feet.

## Potomac Tunnel or the "Old" Harpers Ferry Tunnel

After crossing the power canal bridge, the line passed through the spine of a bluff approximately 1 mile upstream from Harpers Ferry. Dug during 1839-1840, this was the first tunnel completed on the B&O (the railroad completed its Paw Paw tunnel the next year), and just the sixth railroad tunnel yet built in the United States. Originally, the B&O was going to cut through the bluff, but after digging 40-foot-deep cuts on either side, the company opted for a tunnel the remaining distance, reasoning that it added no extra cost to the work. It was a double-track tunnel, 86 feet long by 22 feet high, and three months were required to blast through the hard gneiss using black powder. The tunnel cost $4,386 and never required a lining or formal portals.[43]

## Completion of the Westward Extension to Cumberland in 1842

During 1841 the contractors completed the majority of the "graduation, masonry, and bridging" between Harpers Ferry and Cumberland. By October 1842 only three bridges remained unfinished on the 41 miles between Harpers Ferry and Hancock--one being the new addition to the Harpers Ferry bridge.[44] Most sections east of Hancock were ready for the ballast and track by late 1842. For 10 miles west of Harpers Ferry wooden ties were already in place awaiting the iron rails. Originally the company had hoped for a January 1842 opening, but a shortage of timber in the fall of 1841 delayed completion of some bridges, including the one at Harpers Ferry.[45]

For bridges (such as the government canal span) over 50 feet long on the new line, Latrobe relied on the Latrobian truss, following the form of the Latrobe/Wernwag bridge

*Figure 15-The only known photo of the "old" Harpers Ferry tunnel, ca. 1880. (NPS photo.)*

*Figure 16-This ca. 1855 lithograph shows Harpers Ferry at its pinnacle prior to the Civil War. The configuration of the bridge at lower left is somewhat inaccurate--the locomotive is shown on the turnpike side of the canal span. (Hahn Collection.)*

at Harpers Ferry. Wooden bridges of 50 feet or less were apparently covered deck-trusses of an unknown truss design (i.e. the boatway bridge). Most wooden bridges on the line from Harpers Ferry to Cumberland were covered in clapboard, roofed, and painted to protect them from the elements. Probably at Latrobe's directing, the larger bridges on the line were adorned with neo-classical details, sometimes incorporating doric columns and oversized cornices similar to the Harpers Ferry bridge.

The railroad began opening the line in sections, starting with the 30 miles from Harpers Ferry to Martinsburg which opened on May 21, 1842. Ten days later the main stem opened to Hancock. Work continued for some months on the line west of Hancock, and in the end track crews were laying rails at a rate of 1 mile per day.[46] The line finally opened to Cumberland on December 1, 1842, making that city a ten-hour train ride from Baltimore.

## 1844-1845 Truss Failures

The second span, or wyed span, created to turn the main stem toward the armory wall functioned perfectly for the first two-and-a-half years it was in use. A thorough inspection of the bridge in mid-1844 showed no signs of trouble, and the bridge had been newly "keyed up" (the spans are heavily loaded and wedged into place, so that when the weight is removed the wedges prevent the span from flexing back into position--this "pre-stresses" the

structure). Two weeks after the inspection a truss of the wyed span collapsed without warning under the weight of a single locomotive and tender, dropping them into the river. Fortunately no lives were lost, although it could have been much worse. Eight loaded trains, some carrying passengers, had passed over the same span the previous day without incident. The remaining spans were undamaged and the company soon trestled the gap to restore train service. The B&O later recovered the locomotive, which had only superficial damage.[47]

The subsequent inspection of the bridge revealed the cause to be decay of "several pieces of timber, comprising an important part of the framing of the arch."[48] Decay, which the clapboard siding and roof was meant to eliminate, was the bane of wooden trusses. An inspection in the wake of the accident found that

> indeed the final fracture took place in a part of the frame so situated, and so surrounded and kept in place, as that there could be no sensible yielding without a total giving away. The decay, therefore, most probably proceeding from an unperceived leak in the tin roof and the spreading of the water between the several pieces of timber composing the straining beam, had been progressing silently and unsuspected, until the strength of the remaining sound wood became insufficient to withstand the strain to which it was subjected.[49]

The B&O rebuilt the arch that winter, probably using Latrobe's "improved" truss by this time. In March of 1845, just two months after the wyed span was rebuilt, a coal train was crossing the bridge when the curved span suddenly collapsed, dropping ten coal cars and a caboose into the river. Again there were no major injuries. "The recurrence of such an accident, as will be readily supposed, created the most lively anxiety in the minds of the B&O board, both as to the durability of the bridges along the entire route, and the principle upon which they were constructed."[50] The culprit this time was again claimed to be faulty workmanship and insufficient inspection of the work while the span was under construction, relieving Latrobe of any direct responsibility. The report continued:

> It was also attributable in part to the premature removal, by a sudden flood in the river, of the temporary supports which had been put under the arch during its repair, and for assisting it while deprived of the counter-thrust of the adjacent span, which had not then been reconstructed. It will also be remembered that it was necessary to hasten the finishing of the bridges along the route, in order to avoid delay in the opening of the road to Cumberland and, the difficulty which attended the procuring of the proper description of timber in sufficient quantities, made, in some instances, a very rigid inspection, scarcely practicable....[51]

The curved span was rebuilt at a cost of around $6,000, and Latrobe commented in 1847 that, "All the new work has stood the test of its strengths completely and the most difficult and extensive structure of the whole, the wide arch at Harpers Ferry has now borne the trade of the road under the most trying circumstances for two years without exhibiting the smallest weakness in any of its parts."[52] The first collapse had led to a thorough inspection and reconstruction of nearly every wooden bridge between Harpers Ferry and Cumberland. Only six years old, they were obsolete, "They were built originally with a view to much lighter locomotives and trains than those since traversing the road...."[53] This included the trestlework at Harpers Ferry, and apparently 1,633 feet of the trestle was rebuilt or reinforced with new timbers.

## Here Come the Floods

Beginning in 1843, floods increasingly struck the lower town and routinely put the Potomac bridge in danger. The first, in April of that year, was described as the worst since 1810. A week of rain and melting snows sent the two rivers out of their banks. Water covered the lower streets, and the C&O Canal was extensively damaged. It was the first major test of Latrobe's bridge, and the *Virginia Free Press* reported, "The great Rail Road bridge over the Potomac was in imminent danger, the stream being within 18 inches of the timbers, and the drift-wood in many instances broke off the plank which lined the frame work...."[54] It survived with minor damage, but some were not so lucky. The newspaper mentioned that Wernwag, "whose enterprise and usefulness are proverbial, was a loser to the amount of several hundreds of dollars...."[55]

Two more floods struck in September. The first was caused by continuous heavy rains the night of September 6, and matched the destruction of the April flood. The newspaper lamented, "It seems as if the heavens had been opened, as in the deluge of old...."[56] The second, just two weeks later, occurred after six days of nearly continuous rain, and was 3 feet higher than the April flood and 1 foot higher than in 1810. Boats plied Potomac and Shenandoah Streets, where water was in the first story of many buildings. The *Virginia Free Press* observed that, "The water was touching the Rail Road Bridge, and the rise of another foot must have swept that costly work away."[57] Damage was extensive, "The amount of loss is incalculable, and the two freshets of September will be matters for remembrance for the present generation."[58] Disastrous floods came regularly over the next fifteen years, but the bridge survived them all. It became standard practice during high water to weight the bridge with loaded coal cars to hold the superstructure in place.

## Replacement of the Winchester Span, 1851

The next major improvement to the Latrobe/Wernwag bridge came in 1851 when the B&O's Master of Road, Wendel Bollman, erected a new "Bollman truss" all-iron bridge design to replace the original wooden Winchester span. Bollman's Winchester span was a marvelous structure, combining both cast and wrought iron, and its design helped establish Bollman as a premier figure in civil engineering during the nineteenth century.

## Wendel Bollman's Importance to the Rise of All-Iron Bridges

The limitations of wood, combined with the increasing demands of railroads, pressed civil engineers like Bollman to develop and refine various types of all-iron trusses. Indeed, the needs of railroads spurred the advancement of bridge building technology in the nineteenth century like no other factor. Certainly no other contemporary transportation system needed bridges of such superior strength or durability. Compared to wood, iron spans were largely immune from fire and decay, and able to handle greater loads. On the other hand, iron was plagued by public mistrust and a general lack of understanding of stress analysis. The lack of experience with iron led engineers to refine their methods of calculating stress and strain in order to further unravel iron's physical properties and ensure safer bridges. Wendel Bollman and his contemporaries, such as Squire Whipple and Herman Haupt, worked to instill the rationality of mathematics and science to iron-bridge design at a time when the calculation of structural stresses was still in its infancy.

Compared to wrought iron, cast iron was a relatively inexpensive material, but it was brittle and worked well only in compression. It was easily cast into ornate compression members, or any form desired, although few engineers trusted large castings for bridges and opted for wooden compression members instead. On the other hand, because wrought iron worked well both in tension and compression, it was an ideal material for bridge building. However, it was produced by small-scale shops and labor intensive to create, making it simply too expensive in America for large compression members. Thus, wrought iron was generally formed into long, thin, rod or eye-bar tension members. In the interim between all-wood and all-metal bridges, engineers built many composite structures of wood and iron, such as the Latrobe/Wernwag bridge, with

---

## *Wendel Bollman: A Biographical Sketch*

*Figure 17- Wendel Bollman, ca. 1870.*

Wendel Bollman (1814-1884) was another innovative figure in the engineering field, coming from a traditional carpentry background, but emerging as a leader in the more theoretical, mathematically-based aspects of bridge engineering and the use of iron trusses. Unlike Wernwag or Wever, Bollman was thoroughly modern in his professionalism and reliance on mathematical formulae. Historian Robert Vogel has described Bollman as "perhaps the most successful of the self-taught engineers and probably one of the last. He may be said to be a true representative of the transitional period between intuitive and exact engineering."[59]

Wendel Bollman's acquaintance with Harpers Ferry began early in his life, part of his rather humble upbringing. He was born in Baltimore on January 21, 1814, the son of a German emigrant and baker, the seventh of eight children. He attended Bassford's free school on Courtland Street in Baltimore and a private school, but was largely self-taught in engineering. When Wendel's father died, he left his mother in a poor financial state. So in 1825, around the age of eleven, Wendel went to work in a drugstore run by a family friend in Shepherdstown, Virginia (now West Virginia), 10 miles northwest of Harpers Ferry. "He learned the business very rapidly, having in six months acquired the name in English and Latin of every drug, tincture, and compound in the store. The next year he opened a drugstore at Harpers Ferry, but falling sick [perhaps with cholera, which often ravaged the Potomac valley] he was compelled to return to Baltimore and undergo treatment."[60]

After leaving his Harpers Ferry drugstore and returning to Baltimore to recuperate, the young Bollman joined in the procession through the city streets for the laying of the Baltimore and Ohio Railroad cornerstone.[61] After his recovery, Bollman found a job as carpenter's apprentice on the railroad. During 1829-1830, he became a rodman on a surveying crew under newly-hired Benjamin Latrobe Jr. on the main stem west from Baltimore. Bollman worked for the railroad for only a year before leaving and starting his own successful carpentry business.

In 1837, Bollman returned to Harpers Ferry, building a house "for a son of Bishop Waugh."[62] James Murray, an engineer from the B&O's Road Department, asked Bollman to come back to work for the railroad as foreman of bridges.[63] Bollman accepted, and his first order of duty was rebuilding

cast-iron fittings and wrought-iron rods added to strengthen the span.

Generally, the first successful all-iron bridges in this country were based on the arch, not the truss. The very first all-iron bridge in the country, the 1839 Dunlap Creek Bridge at Brownsville, Pennsylvania, on the National Road, carried its load on cast-iron arches. Some engineers relied on more imaginative use of the arch, such as the Whipple iron-bowstring arch, patented in 1841. All-iron trusses began as updated versions of older wooden-truss designs, such as the Town or Howe trusses, and were first patented in the early 1840s. Engineer Richard Osborne erected America's first all-iron truss in 1845 on the Reading Railroad at Manayunk, Pennsylvania, using a wrought-iron Howe truss. Iron bridges did not catch on quickly though, and by 1850 the country possessed only a handful of all-iron spans. In Britain, where the world's first all-iron bridge originated in 1779, the development of iron bridges had followed a different course, partly because of the availability of capital and a mature iron industry that could supply large cast- and wrought-iron bridge mem-

*Figure 18-The Bollman truss in its ca. 1852 form. (IHTIA, drawing by author.)*

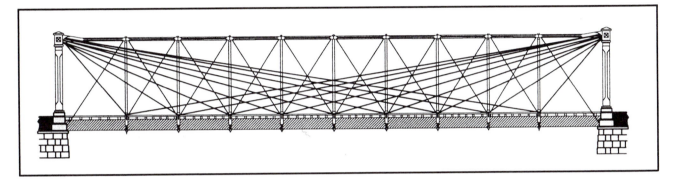

the wyed span on the Latrobe/Wernwag bridge. This time he remained with the company, building bridges, tunnels, and wayside structures for over twenty years. His most significant works were not with wood, however, but with iron.

During the 1840s, Bollman worked his way up though the engineering department under the guidance of Benjamin Latrobe Jr., and was appointed as the B&O's first "master of road" in 1848.[64] This position (which he held for ten years) put all the B&O's tracks, buildings, tunnels, and bridges under his care. Most importantly, Latrobe gave Bollman the time and resources to increase his knowledge of iron's physical properties and develop a new truss design. In 1851-1852, when the B&O was building the final link of the main stem between Cumberland and Wheeling, Latrobe boldly decided to use iron bridges. He adopted the Bollman truss as the B&O's standard iron bridge design around 1852, and the Fink truss soon after that. Both of these iron-truss designs came at a critical time for the railroad as the original wooden bridges on the line's older sections needed replaced because of their age and the increasing size, weight, and speed of trains. After the first Bollman truss was successfully erected in 1851, the B&O's iron foundries at Mt. Clare in Baltimore were expanded to handle the increased number and size of castings required for the main stem's new bridges. The Bollman truss became the world's first standardized, prefabricated, all-iron truss, and made its inventor famous.

Bollman made groundbreaking use of the material in many types of structures, only a few of which are mentioned here. In the mid-1850s, while supervising the lining of the B&O's numerous tunnels, he developed a cast-iron lining system that was safer and easier to erect than the usual brick arch--the first such use of iron tunnel lining in this country. In 1858, Bollman and two of his assistants, John Tegmeyer and James Clark, left the B&O to start their own bridge company in Canton, Maryland, just west of Baltimore. It was among the earliest bridge building companies in the United States, and it specialized in Bollman trusses. At first called W. Bollman and Company, after the Civil War the name changed to the Patapsco Bridge Company. The company fabricated bridges at its own shops and, once disassembled, the bridges could be shipped nearly anywhere. Aside from the bridges on the B&O's lines, Bollman's company built two large bridges in Chile, several in Cuba, and around 1863 built the first all-metal bridge in Mexico near Vera Cruz.[65] One of his most difficult engineering jobs was spanning the Cape Fear River (in North Carolina). During 1867-1868, Bollman sank two cast-iron cylinders, or pneumatic caissons, into the riverbed some 80 feet below the water's surface, "This was one of the first instances of the use of the process in America."[66] He also built a cast-iron framework in 1873 for the dome on Baltimore City Hall.

Bollman's acquaintance with Harpers Ferry continued throughout his career, and he built other structures here for the railroad. After the Civil War the Harpers Ferry bridge would become the most intriguing Bollman span ever built. He remained active in his bridge business, but also became president of the Western Maryland Railway Company (ironically, a competitor to the B&O) and participated in various civil engineering societies. Wendel Bollman died in Baltimore, the city which had supported so many of his works, on March 14, 1884.[67]

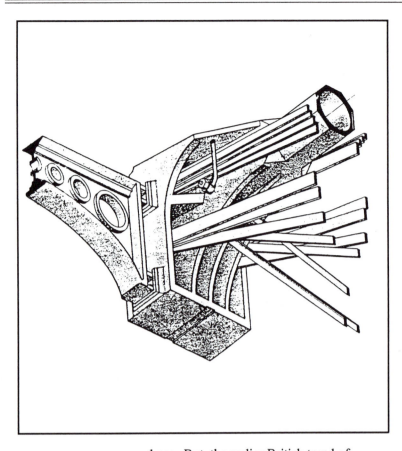

*Figure 19-A detail of a Bollman truss showing where the wrought-iron diagonals connected to the cast-iron tower cap. Note the ornate cast-iron portal and hollow cast-iron top chord (or stretcher). This is a drawing of the 1868 Bollman Winchester span, which replaced Bollman's first Winchester span. (Historic American Engineering Record, drawing by Samuel Gains, Brian Bartholomew, and Joanna Downs, 1987.)*

The permanent principle in bridge building, sustained throughout this mode of structure and in which there is such gain in competition with every other, viz: the direct transfer of weight to the abutments renders the calculation simple, the expense certain, and facilitates the erection of secure, economical, and durable structures.[68]

Latrobe's approval of Bollman's truss for standard use on the B&O main stem marks the full-fledged arrival of iron railroad bridges in America.

## Details on the Bollman Truss Arrangement

While Bollman may have begun developing his unique truss arrangement during the 1840s, he did not receive a patent until January 6, 1852.[69] The design used a combination of cast and wrought iron, reflecting the nature of each metal--cast iron in the compression members and wrought iron in the tension members. This was "the proper condition of the two metals...," said Bollman.[70] Bollman trusses were a remarkable sight, distinguished by the web of wrought-iron diagonals radiating from the top of granite end towers. Although complicated in appearance, they were simple to erect. Numbers were cast into each piece for easy identification and each bridge was test assembled at the B&O's shops, disassembled, and taken to the bridge site. They could be erected with greater ease and required fewer skilled laborers than either wooden or masonry bridges.

The essential load-bearing members of the Bollman truss were the wrought-iron bars. Wrought-iron tension members had been used on bridges for at least thirty years. James Finley's wrought-iron chain suspension bridges were, perhaps, the most extreme examples. But chain or wire-rope suspension bridges were considered to lack the rigidity required for railroad use and were used only in special instances, such as Roebling's railroad bridge across the Niagara completed in 1855. Otherwise, in most structures

bers. But, the earlier British trend of building masonry railroad viaducts or large embankments in lieu of wooden bridges had stymied the development of wooden--and consequently iron--truss arrangements. While far ahead of the United States in monumental iron bridges by 1850, the British had done comparatively little toward developing a wide range of iron truss designs. Engineers like Robert Stephenson were building massive all-iron bridges, but these were generally based either on the arch, or otherwise giant, hollow box girders--not intricate truss arrangements (there were exceptions, but these were rare). In America however, the plethora of wooden truss designs led to a similar variety of all-iron trusses. Here, engineers like Bollman advanced the use of all-iron bridges, but were concerned less with monumental bridges as the creation of shorter spans that were cheap, efficient, and safe. The Bollman truss was the epitome of this ideal for many years. In summarizing his patented design, Bollman noted:

wrought-iron members had been limited to secondary roles (such as the vertical rods supporting the deck on the Latrobian truss) while the primary load-bearing members were wooden compression members. This was where Bollman's design--relying on the long, wrought-iron bars acting under tension to carry the load--differed from most other trusses. This arrangement was called a *suspension truss*, and it combined the principles of the suspension bridge and the standard rigid truss into a form acceptable for railroad use.

The main wrought-iron diagonals worked in combination with a simple underlying truss layout formed of vertical cast-iron posts and a horizontal cast-iron top chord, or "stretcher" as Bollman called it, working under compression, with two secondary wrought-iron diagonals within each panel. Yet, this underlying truss was practically non-load bearing and acted mainly to stiffen the bridge. Most of the load was actually carried di-

rectly back to the tops of the end towers by the independently acting wrought-iron bars. This made the lower chord superfluous, and in the deck version it was often omitted altogether. The main diagonals were hung from the cast-iron tower caps by wrought-iron pins, which transferred the load vertically down through the end towers and into the masonry abutments. As Bollman explained:

> The stretcher or straining beam, the vertical posts, and suspension bars compose the essential features of the bridge-each post being hung by two bars from both ends of the stretcher independently of all the others; and each post and pair of tension bars forming with the stretcher a separate truss.[71]

In other words, the truss isolated each panel, so that one or more suspension diagonals could fail without affecting the remainder of the bridge. A safety feature, it also allowed comparatively easy repairs. Bollman wrote:

*Figure 20-This drawing of the 1868 Bollman Winchester span clearly shows the configuration of the wrought-iron suspension bars. The drawing also identifies parts of the truss recovered from the Potomac River in recent years. (Historic American Engineering Record, drawing by Samuel Gains, Brian Bartholomew, and Joanna Downs, 1987.)*

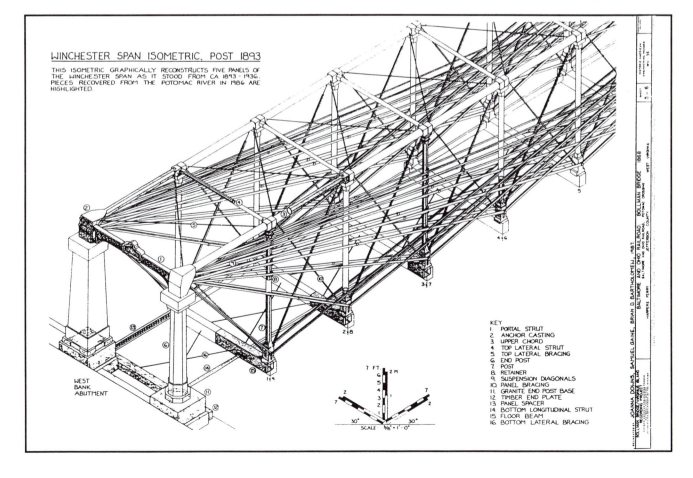

WINCHESTER SPAN ISOMETRIC, POST 1893

THIS ISOMETRIC GRAPHICALLY RECONSTRUCTS FIVE PANELS OF THE WINCHESTER SPAN AS IT STOOD FROM CA 1893 - 1936. PIECES RECOVERED FROM THE POTOMAC RIVER IN 1986 ARE HIGHLIGHTED.

WEST BANK ABUTMENT

KEY
1. PORTAL STRUT
2. ANCHOR CASTING
3. UPPER CHORD
4. TOP LATERAL STRUT
5. TOP LATERAL BRACING
6. END POST
7. POST
8. RETAINER
9. SUSPENSION DIAGONALS
10. PANEL BRACING
11. GRANITE END POST BASE
12. TIMBER END PLATE
13. PANEL SPACER
14. BOTTOM LONGITUDINAL STRUT
15. FLOOR BEAM
16. BOTTOM LATERAL BRACING

Should a new floor beam be required, it is but needed to slacken the horizontal rod and the keys in [the] longitudinal strut, remove the washer under [the] point of suspension, and let down the beam to be replaced; which can be done without trustling [sic] up any part of the bridge.[72]

The wrought-iron suspension bars were relatively easy to make, and were adjustable. According to Bollman:

The rods from the centre to abutments [have] but an eye at one, and a screw at the other, end; with a weld or two between according to length. The long counter rods have two knuckles and one swivel for adjustment of strain, and convenience in welding, as well as in raising the whole.[73]

The transverse floor beams were riveted box girders with a cast-iron top and bottom and wrought-iron sides. Both the top and bottom chords were tied together with wrought-iron lateral bracing rods and cast-iron struts. Bollman bridges had decorative cast-iron portal transoms identifying (among other things) himself as the patent holder and the year of fabrication.[74]

In his early tests for the design Bollman had used wood for the compression members, but soon he incorporated a new structural member he had invented to replace both the wooden verticals and wooden stretchers. It was a hollow, "octagonal without, circular within" cast-iron structural member, and its use made Bollman's all-iron truss possible.[75] The cast iron averaged 1 inch in thickness, making the columns both light and strong, and less likely to hide major casting flaws than a solid member. As top chord stretchers they were made in sections and connected to the vertical posts by mortise-and-tenon joints.[76] Bollman's hollow columns were the forerunner of the *Phoenix column*, a similarly hollow--although wrought-iron--structural member which Bollman created during the mid-1850s. Iron shops could not supply wrought-iron members large enough to use as compression members, so Bollman used curved sections of rolled wrought iron (with standing flanges so the segments could be riveted together) to create hollow col-

umns. Although Bollman never used Phoenix columns on Bollman trusses, the invention was later patented and manufactured by the Phoenix Bridge Company and gained great popularity.

The Bollman truss was considered an all-iron bridge, but nonetheless it incorporated a considerable amount of wood for stringers and crossties. Also, roofed wooden boxes covered the top of each abutment tower to protect the multitude of connections at that point. Still, the independently-acting diagonals prevented major damage from fire, "In case of fire, the floor may be entirely consumed without any injury to the side truss," wrote Bollman.[77]

Bollman gradually strengthened certain portions of the design after 1852. The end towers, granite on the first three Bollman trusses, were changed to cast iron on later versions to simplify erection. The portals and structural members of post-Civil War Bollman trusses were made more substantial than those built before the war, and flanges were cast into the stretchers to increase their strength.[78]

How did Bollman originally develop his truss design? There is a precursor to the Bollman truss, from which Bollman derived his particular design in the middle to late 1840s. Historian Robert Vogel described it as:

A basic technique commonly used to increase the capacity of a simple timber beam--that of trussing--i.e., placing beneath the beam a rod of iron that was anchored at the ends of the beam and held a certain distance below it at the center by a vertical strut or post.[79]

While using such simple trussed beams for short spans, Bollman probably realized that by multiplying the iron rods and vertical posts the span could be lengthened considerably. The incorporation of iron into the design was only logical, especially considering the influence of Latrobe. It is also possible that Bollman found inspiration for his truss in Latrobe's bridge designs. Vogel points out that an illustration of a Bollman truss, if inverted, suddenly resembles a Latrobian truss--like that of the Latrobe/Wernwag Bridge at Harpers Ferry! Was the Latrobian truss Bollman's inspiration for the design? Similar in appearance, they are functionally reversed. The diagonal arch-braces of the Latrobian truss were compression members, while the diagonal bars of the Bollman truss were suspension (or tension) members. Yet both truss designs *were* similar in that they consisted of numerous independently acting trusses, where the failure of one would not affect the remainder. There are other intriguing questions about the design, as the Bollman truss also closely resembles another suspension truss developed at nearly the same time by his colleague on the B&O, Albert Fink. There are some lingering questions over the origins of Bollman's design that may never be answered.

The B&O began building Bollman trusses in earnest after 1852, reaching an apex in the years just after the Civil War. They could be found all along the B&O's original main stem, in both deck- and through-truss versions, having replaced many of Latrobe's wooden bridges. The B&O probably erected over one hundred Bollman trusses on the main stem and its various branches during the three decades it was used.[80] While the Bollman truss became popular on the B&O, it was not widely used by other railroads.

Among the last, and probably the largest, bridges on which Bollman trusses were used were the B&O's two Ohio River crossings: the bridge from Benwood, West Virginia, to Bellaire, Ohio; and a similar structure built downriver, crossing from Parkersburg, West Virginia, to Belpre, Ohio. The Benwood bridge (finished in 1871) used nine Bollman deck trusses from 106 feet to 108 feet long, and a combination of six Linville and Piper trusses from 209 feet to 350 feet long at mid-river to form a continuous iron bridge 1,435 feet long with an equally long masonry approach viaduct.[81] The Parkersburg bridge (also finished in 1871) was similar in form, but incorpo-

rated an incredible twenty-eight Bollman deck spans.

The Bollman truss design also had certain inherent problems which helped lead to its eventual demise. For one thing it used more iron than other bridge trusses of comparable strength. Moreover, the variety of diagonal lengths responded unevenly to temperature changes and needed constant readjustment.[82] Most problematic, in longer spans (over 100 feet) the longest diagonal rods were almost horizontal, lessening their effectiveness and causing an unacceptable deflection under heavy loads. This factor kept Bollman trusses from reaching lengths much greater than 150 feet. This is graphically illustrated by the Benwood/Bellaire bridge, whereby Bollman trusses could only be used in the shorter (108 feet) approach spans while the mid-river spans (350 feet) were modified Whipple trusses. In the early 1850s, however, the Bollman truss was completely satisfactory for the B&O's needs.

As time went on the B&O used Bollman trusses less and less in favor of the Fink truss, which used less iron and performed better. Other railroads preferred the Fink as well. The B&O constructed Bollman trusses from 1850 to about 1875, when the increasing weight of rolling stock finally made the Bollman design obsolete, though use of the Fink truss continued slightly longer. New all-steel designs took the place of both the Bollman and Fink truss for railroad bridges after 1890 (the Fink truss had continued success as a roof truss, and can still be seen in buildings today). Some Bollman truss bridges remained in use into the twentieth century, reinforced with structural steel to give them a few more years of service. In the end, Bollman was respected as one of the fathers of the iron-truss bridge. As Vogel wrote, "the soundness of his designs and the excellence of the workmanship carried out under his direction, are attested by the fact that a number of his bridges performed useful service as railway structures for four score years."[83]

## The Bollman Winchester Span

Before choosing Bollman's truss for use on the main stem from Cumberland to Wheeling, the company tested the design by erecting spans at three separate locations. In 1849, the B&O erected the first Bollman truss at Savage, Maryland, across the Little Patuxent River. This single, 76-foot-long span carried an industrial spur (off the B&O's Washington Branch) across the Little Patuxent River to the Savage Factory textile mill. Ironically, the only known remaining Bollman truss bridge sits adjacent to the spot where the first was built in 1849. This two-span Bollman was built after the Civil War for use somewhere on the B&O's lines, and moved to the location it now occupies ca. 1887.[84]

The original Bollman truss at Savage performed well, and in 1851 Latrobe decided to erect Bollman trusses at Bladensburg, Maryland, and Harpers Ferry. Both the Savage and Bladensburg spans were less than 80 feet long, while the Harpers Ferry Winchester span, 124 feet long, was by far the largest Bollman truss up to that time. The B&O strategically chose the Winchester plan for replacement. The Latrobe/Wernwag bridge was some fifteen years old, and its ongoing problems left little to lose with a brand new, albeit somewhat experimental, span. It would be Bollman's--and the B&O's--showpiece. Bollman took the trouble to produce a pamphlet discussing the finer points of the bridge, providing basic stress diagrams to support his (and the railroad's) confidence in the design. It is a revealing document, showing how far Bollman had advanced his mathematical stress calculations and his understanding of iron's properties. He was becoming quite a salesman as well.

With its light, airy appearance and lack of covering, the iron Winchester span was an odd-looking addition to the rest of the bridge. The B&O's 1851 *Annual Report* mentions the new iron Winchester Span, and touches on the impact of heavier locomotives on the company's old wooden bridges:

> That part of the Bridge at Harper's Ferry, known as the Winchester Span, has been so far completed as to be brought into full use, and has cost $6,743.49. It is a very substantial iron structure, from which most permanent service may be expected. Material repairs have been also completed on some of the wooden bridges, which makes them more reliable than before for the heavy engines which now prevail on the road.[85]

The Winchester span's truss arrangement consisted of three parallel truss lines, 128 feet long. Each truss had eight panels, with seven vertical compression members supported by seven pairs of suspension bars hung from each end tower.[86] Bollman received the patent for his truss

*Figure 21 & 22-Details on the original Winchester Bollman span and (below) an elevation of the Potomac bridge as it appeared from 1852 to 1861. Drawing not to scale. (Measurements and weights from Wendel Bollman, Iron Suspension and Trussed Bridge..., 1852, p. 2; drawing by author.)*

| Clear Span | Truss Length | Weight of Cast Iron | Weight of Wrought Iron | Total Weight of Bridge Iron |
|------------|--------------|---------------------|------------------------|-----------------------------|
| 124' | 128' | 65,137 lbs | 33,3527 lbs | 98,664 lbs. |

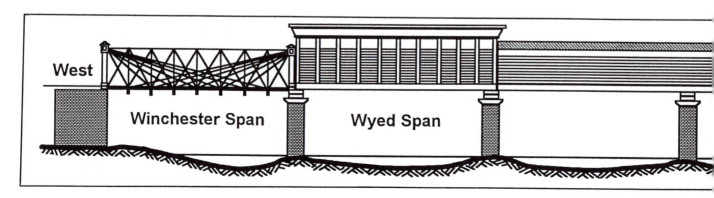

West

Winchester Span

Wyed Span

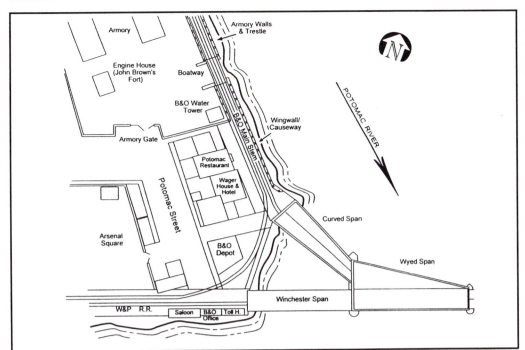

*Figure 23-A map depicting the area at the west end of the B&O bridge, ca. 1859, just prior to John Brown's raid and the Civil War. (IHTIA, drawing by author.)*

design on January 6, 1852, shortly after completing the Winchester Span.

After Bollman finished the bridge, the company carried out a series of tests. Gauges were placed at the center and ends of the trusses. Then, "three first class tonnage engines with three tenders, were first carefully weighed, and then run upon the bridge, at the same time nearly covering its whole length, and weighing an aggregate 273,550 lbs., ...being over a ton for each foot in length of the bridge."[87] With the engines moving at 8 miles an hour, the bridge deflected one-and three-eighths inches, and at the first vertical post out from the abutments the bridge deflected nine-sixteenths of an inch, both satisfactory.[88]

The Potomac bridge existed in this hybrid form for the next eight years, during which time some of the best-known photos of it were taken. Incredibly, this one bridge had come to represent three significant persons in nineteenth-century engineering (Wernwag, Latrobe, and Bollman), each of whom represents distinct periods in the evolution of American civil engineering. It seems as if fate brought these three great builders together at Harpers Ferry.

## Rebuilding the Armory Trestlework

The trestlework along the armory wall was replaced in-kind with a cast-and wrought-iron version between 1853 and 1858.[89] Bollman probably designed the trestle's ironwork, although there is no direct evidence. Yet, there is good reason to credit Bollman because in 1851 he had designed and built a street trestle over the

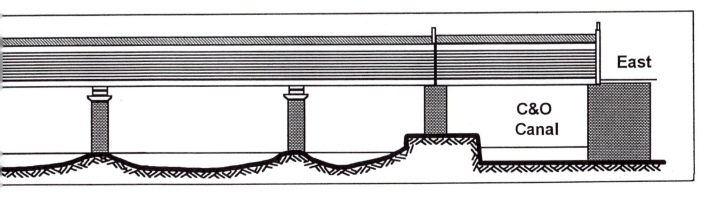

main stem in Baltimore which incorporated wooden bents tied together with wrought-iron diagonals, the nation's first use of iron in a trestle.[90] In 1852, fellow B&O engineer Albert Fink had designed the very first all-iron trestles in the United States for the crossing of Tray Run and Buckeye Run in the mountains of Preston County, (West) Virginia, and those too rested on masonry walls. But compared to the Harpers Ferry trestle, Tray and Buckeye viaducts were much taller and differed in form.

While Fink's viaducts used hollow, inclined cast-iron bents (or legs), the Harpers Ferry trestle bents were vertical.[91] The cap piece was a fishbelly-shaped, cast-iron girder approximately 3 feet deep and 20 feet wide, and pierced by five round holes. Most likely, wrought-iron rods connected diagonally across the width of each bent, and cast-iron beams served as stringers between bents, supporting the crossties and rails. Cast-iron handrails along either side of the trestle connected to the cap pieces. Wood decking covered the trestle most of its length. The bridges located along the trestlework were probably replaced with Bollman deck spans at this time. One-third of the trestle was finished by 1854, and by the end of 1855 the reconstruction had cost $13,768.71. Another $3,589.91 was spent to complete the work in early 1857.[92] The rebuilt Harpers Ferry trestle was the third all-iron trestle erected in America.

## The Water Tower

During 1856 the B&O built a rectangular, Italianate-style water tower within the northeast corner of the armory grounds. Wendel Bollman designed the approximately 17 by 17-foot-square, 40-foot-tall brick water tower and masked its function by mimicking the other armory buildings. It supplied a water-siphon (for locomotives) which pierced the decking near the west end of the Potomac bridge, and was also a fire safety measure protecting the bridge and trestle. The Secretary of War, Jefferson Davis, in agreeing to let the B&O build this structure reserved the

government's right to demand its demolition at any time.[93] The government would never have to, as it would not stand long.

The 1850s had been a golden era for the B&O railroad. The completion of the main stem to Wheeling, (West) Virginia, on Christmas Eve of 1852, and subsequent extensions westward boded well for the company. In passing the Appalachians, the railroad also opened up a vast coal producing region for development, and it quickly became the major commodity hauled by the B&O. The clouds of war were on the horizon, however, and events would soon rivet the nation's eyes on Harpers Ferry.

## Notes

1. *Virginia Free Press*, September 10, 1835, 2.

2. Ibid., 3.

3. *Baltimore and Ohio Railroad Ninth Annual Report, 1835*, 112.

4. Ibid.

5. The letter designations are from the Historic American Engineering Record drawings of the 1868 Bollman truss Winchester span.

6. *B&O Railroad Bridge Piers Stabilization Design Project: Assessment Data and Treatment Recommendations Report*, 18.

7. Ibid., 34.

8. As quoted in Dilts, *The Great Road*, 218, from the B.H. Latrobe Jr., Journal, MS Gamble Collection, Maryland Historical Society.

9. *Baltimore and Ohio Railroad Tenth Annual Report, 1835*, 3.

10. As quoted in Dilts, *The Great Road*, 218, from the B.H. Latrobe Jr., Journal, MS Gamble Collection, Maryland Historical Society.

11. *Baltimore and Ohio Railroad Tenth Annual Report, 1835*, 3.

12. *Virginia Free Press*, October 20, 1836, 2.

13. *Virginia Free Press*, January 26, 1837, 2.

14. Dilts, *The Great Road*, 219.

15. *Baltimore and Ohio Railroad Eleventh Annual Report, 1837*, 28-29.

16. Ibid.

17. Ibid., 10.

18. *Baltimore and Ohio Railroad Twelfth Annual Report, 1838*, 15.

19. Gilbert, *Where Industry Failed...*, 40.

20. *Baltimore and Ohio Railroad Twenty-First Annual Report, 1847*, 37.

21. Gilbert, 41.

22. *Baltimore and Ohio Railroad Tenth Annual Report, 1836*, 3.

23. Ibid., 88.

24. Ibid., 15.

25. Smith, *The Book of the Great Railway Celebrations of 1857*, 33-34.

26. *Baltimore and Ohio Railroad Tenth Annual Report, 1836*, 53.

27. *Baltimore and Ohio Railroad Thirteenth Annual Report, 1839*, 6.

28. *Baltimore and Ohio Railroad Tenth Annual Report, 1836*, 59.

29. *Baltimore and Ohio Railroad Eleventh Annual Report, 1837*, 20. 59.

30. *Baltimore and Ohio Railroad Twelfth Annual Report, 1838*, 10.

31. Smith, *The Book of the Great Railway Celebrations of 1857*, 36.

32. *Baltimore and Ohio Railroad Twelfth Annual Report, 1838*, 11.

33. *Baltimore and Ohio Railroad Thirteenth Annual Report, 1839*, 7.

34. Snell, "Historic Building Site Survey Report for Wager Lot 1 and the Bridge Lot...," National Park Service, Harpers Ferry National Historical Park, September 22, 1958, 22.

35. Smith, 151.

36. Snell, 23.

37. National Archives, Record Group 121, Public Buildings Service. Harpers Ferry Laminated Material.

38. *Virginia Free Press*, November 28, 1839, 2.

39. *Baltimore and Ohio Railroad Thirty-Second Annual Report, 1858*, 130-131.

40. National Archives, Record Group 121, Public Buildings Service. Harpers Ferry Laminated Material.

41. *Baltimore and Ohio Railroad Thirty-Second Annual Report, 1858*, 131.

42. Ibid.

43. Drinker, *Tunneling, Explosive Compounds, and Rock Drills*, 1064.

44. *Baltimore and Ohio Railroad Fifteenth Annual Report, 1841*, 10.

45. *Baltimore and Ohio Railroad Sixteenth Annual Report, 1842*, 8.

46. Snell, 42-43.

47. Ibid.

48. Ibid., 5.

49. *Baltimore and Ohio Railroad Nineteenth Annual Report, 1845*, 10-11.

50. Ibid.

51. *Baltimore and Ohio Railroad Twenty-First Annual Report, 1847*, 37-38.

52. Ibid.

53. *Virginia Free Press*, April 20, 1843, 2.

54. Ibid.

55. *Virginia Free Press*, September 14, 1843, 2.

56. Ibid., September 21, 1843, 2.

57. Ibid.

58. Ibid.

59. Vogel, "The Engineering Contributions of Wendel Bollman," 82.

60. Anonymous, "The Late Wendel Bollman," 200.

61. Ibid.

62. Ibid.

63. Ibid.

64. Lee, *A Biographical Dictionary of American Engineers*, 12.

65. Anonymous, "The Late Wendel Bollman," 200.

66. Lee, 12.

67. Anonymous, "The Late Wendel Bollman," 200.

68. Bollman, *Iron Suspension and Trussed Bridge as Constructed for the Baltimore and Ohio Railroad Company at Harper's Ferry, and on the Washington Branch of this Road*, 8.

69. Bollman, "Construction of Bridges," U.S. Patent No. 8,624, January 6, 1852.

70. Bollman, *Iron Suspension and Trussed Bridge...Constructed for the Baltimore and Ohio Railroad Company at Harper's Ferry*, 6.

71. Ibid., 2.

72. Ibid., 8.

73. Ibid., 2.

74. Vogel, "Speculations on the History and Original Appearance of the Last Bollman Truss," 431.

75. Bollman, *Iron Suspension and Trussed Bridge...Constructed for the Baltimore and Ohio Railroad Company at Harper's Ferry*, 2.

76. Ibid.

77. Ibid., 8.

78. Vogel, "Speculations on the History and Original Appearance of the Last Bollman Truss," 431.

79. Vogel, "The Engineering Contributions of Wendel Bollman," 88.

80. Vogel, "Speculations on the History and Original Appearance of the Last Bollman Truss," 429.

81. Greiner, "The American Railroad Viaduct, Its Origin and Evolution," 146.

82. Vogel, "The Engineering Contributions of Wendel Bollman," 90.

83. Anonymous, "A Milestone in Bridge Design," 138.

84. Vogel, "Speculations on the History and Original Appearance of the Last Bollman Truss," 429.

85. Baltimore and Ohio Railroad Board of Directors, Minute Book G, Baltimore and Ohio Railroad Museum.

86. Vogel, "The Engineering Contributions of Wendel Bollman," 89.

87. Bollman, *Iron Suspension and Trussed Bridge...Constructed for the Baltimore and Ohio Railroad Company at Harper's Ferry*, 10.

88. Ibid.

89. *Baltimore and Ohio Railroad Twenty-Seventh Annual Report, 1853*, 247.

90. Greiner, 350.

91. Concluded from photographic evidence.

92. *Baltimore and Ohio Railroad Twenty-Ninth Annual Report, 1855*, 43; and, *Baltimore and Ohio Railroad Thirty-First Annual Report, 1857*, 11.

93. Snell, 37.

# PART FOUR:

# John Brown's Raid, the Civil War, and Post-War Rebuilding: 1859-1893

*Figure 1-One of the best, but probably last, photos of the Potomac bridge prior to the Civil War, ca. 1859. Events swirled around the span during John Brown's raid. Note the Bollman Winchester span, and the trackside water tower in the armory grounds on the lower left. Brown's "Fort" is just out of view. (NPS photo.)*

## John Brown's Raid and the Civil War

John Brown's October 1859 raid on Harpers Ferry marked a turning point in American history. It lit a tinderbox of animosity which had been building for the previous half-century, and the flames of war eventually swept the nation for four long years. Railroads played a major role in warfare for the first time in history, and in turn were wantonly destroyed for the first time. These great internal improvements which had taken so long to construct were now mere pawns in a much larger game. Railroad bridges were particular focal points of destruction, since in addition to trains they could be used by foot troops and wagons, and they took

time and resources to replace. But nothing was spared: depots, roundhouses, tunnels, water tanks, tracks and ties, locomotives, and rolling stock were all subject to destruction.

At Harpers Ferry, the B&O was involved in events from the very outset. When John Brown's raiding party descended on the town the night of October 16, they first captured the B&O's bridge watchman, William Williams, near the Maryland side. He was the first of over forty prisoners to be taken to the armory's fire engine house, Brown's makeshift fort, which sat at the southern end of the armory. Brown left his son, Oliver, and another man to guard the bridge while he and his party crossed into Harpers Ferry

*"The fact that it is the seat of a national armory, and has been described in glowing language by Jefferson, may have given it a wider notoriety than the comparative merits of its scenery would justify..."*
*--Harpers New Monthly Magazine, June, 1859.[1]*

to take the armory and arsenal. The railroad bridge was Brown's only real escape route back to Maryland, and he needed to hold it. Around midnight, the bridge guards captured Patrick Higgins coming from his Sandy Hook home to relieve Williams. While being walked through the bridge to the armory engine house, he managed to break free from his captors and escaped into a hotel along the passenger platform at the bridge's west end.[2]

Soon after, an east-bound train arrived and was stopped by Brown at the platform. Heyward Shepherd, a free African-American employed by the B&O as a baggage handler, made his way from the depot to see why the train had paused. Upon being told to halt by the bridge guards he turned to run, and was shot in the back and killed. Brown ordered the passenger train to proceed, but the conductor waited until daylight fearing that the bridge had been sabotaged. Then, to convince the conductor of the bridge's safety, Brown walked him across the bridge ahead of the train.[3] Once across, the train steamed away and carried the news of the raid to the outside world.

Around noon that day, the Jefferson Guards, a militia unit from Charles Town, captured the bridge and drove the raiders

into the armory. One raider they captured was taken out on the bridge, shot, and thrown into the Potomac. As the fighting raged, the mayor of Harpers Ferry, Fontain Beckham, was killed while peering around the corner of Bollman's water tower.[3] When Colonel Robert E. Lee and his brigade arrived from Washington to subdue the raiders later that evening, they marched into Harpers Ferry across the B&O's bridge, and captured Brown and his companions.[4]

The coming war would devastate Harpers Ferry. The B&O's main stem traversed the contentious border region between North and South, and whoever controlled it held an upper hand in the war. The North controlled the line for most of the conflict, though the South was able to disrupt operations and destroy large parts of the line on numerous occasions.

The B&O would play a key role in the creation of West Virginia and the incorporation of the Eastern Panhandle into the new state. These counties had traditionally identified more with the piedmont of Virginia than the mountainous regions to the west, but the B&O was a key supply line which made it essential that the Union keep this region under control. Aside from being the home of the armory and arsenal, Harpers Ferry commanded the northern entrance to the Shenandoah Valley, the "breadbasket of the Confederacy." So Harpers Ferry became a supremely strategic location in the Civil War, although it proved to be nearly undefendable and repeatedly changed hands. The war officially started on April 12, 1861, with the shelling of Fort Sumter. Harpers Ferry was thereafter ravaged by both sides, beginning with the arsenal, which retreating Union troops burned on April 18.

Upon the North's retreat, southern troops occupied Harpers Ferry and much of the B&O's line from Martinsburg to Point of Rocks. The rebels allowed train operations to go on with only minor interference, but this did not last. On June 14, 1861, the Confederates retreated from Harpers Ferry after controlling the town for

*Figure 2-An illustration from Harper's Weekly depicting the destruction of the B&O's bridge on June 14, 1861. (From Harper's Weekly, July 6, 1861, p. 429.)*

nearly a month. Before leaving they blew up the great Latrobe/Wernwag bridge, and burned the woodwork on the armory trestle.

> From the first, preparations had been made for the destruction of the railroad bridge under the superintendence of competent engineers and, early in the morning...the town was alarmed at hearing a loud explosion and seeing the debris of the destroyed bridge flying high in the air.[5]

The engineers did their job well, although Bollman's iron Winchester span remained a little worse for wear but essentially intact. The bridge piers and abutments remained, but the rest of the bridge was wrecked.

through the charred deck and into the Potomac, but the iron trusses still stood.[7]

Repair crews began work on a temporary river trestle in August of 1861, but it could not be completed before Union troops retreated on August 19. Union forces soon retook the area, but on September 29, 1861, the trestlework erected up to August 19 was carried off in a flood, leaving only the two sections adjoining the Maryland shore.[8] After this, the Union forces erected a pontoon bridge across the Potomac on numerous occasions to insure a crossing for troops and supplies. The pontoon bridge met the west shore at the boatway, where

*Figure 3-(Left) A view from the east abutment showing the remains of the B&O's bridge after its destruction. Bollman's Winchester span still stands at the far end of the bridge. (NPS photo.) Figure 4-(Top) Confederate raiders returned a week later--a Winan's Camel locomotive in the Potomac beneath the Winchester span. Figure 5-(Bottom) Mississippians running railroad cars off the wyed-span abutment and into the Potomac. (From Harper's Weekly, July 20, 1861, p. 455.)*

> The whole structure seemed to ignite at once and was soon consumed, the incombustible parts, iron rails and metal roofing, falling into the water, the quantity of half-burned timber there forming a dam the whole way over that one might cross upon.[6]

A week later, Confederate raiders burned the wood flooring and crossties on the Bollman truss and ran a locomotive

troops could pass through the B&O's river wall. The railroad remained severed through the winter, and it would become the longest break in service ever experienced during the railroad's history in Harpers Ferry.

On February 7, 1862, Union forces did their part in the destruction, completing the ruination of the railroad's property in the town.

United States forces under Col. Geary crossed over into Harpers Ferry and burned the Company's hotel, warehouse, ticket office and water station; also, 38 panels, 570 feet in length, of wood work on the double track iron trestling through the arsenal yard and boatway bridge. This was the remainder of the Company's property in Harpers Ferry not destroyed by the enemy.[9]

The line needed to be entirely rebuilt in and around Harpers Ferry, and in early spring repair crews started the job at a frantic pace. On March 4, 1862, crews converged on Harpers Ferry in an attempt to replace the Potomac bridge. With the river flooded and too high to work in, they turned to the iron trestle along the arsenal grounds. The woodwork had been burned and the hand railing removed, but most of the ironwork remained. The two short bridges incorporated into the trestle, tilt hammer bridge and boatway bridge, had been destroyed and required temporary trestlework. Workmen replaced the timber, crossties, and track along the entire 1,620-foot-long section. This was an especially difficult task because much of the iron work and timber had to come from the east and the B&O's foundries at Mount Clare. Without the bridge in place to carry supplies across, no work could be done west of the Potomac crossing. Despite heroic attempts to set the trestle bents in the swift and deep water, crews successfully erected only one on March 5.[10] Instead, crews strung heavy cables across the Potomac and ferried ironwork, timber, crossties, rails, spikes, and track fixtures to the west shore. They finally put a trestle across the Potomac and opened the line on March 12, 1862, allowing trains to enter Harpers Ferry for the first time in nearly nine months.[11]

After all that work, mother nature again set about a course of destruction. In mid-April 1862, the floods came again, and the company ran loaded coal cars out on the Potomac trestle to help hold it in place. They were not enough, and on the morning of April 22, 1862, the three eastern spans washed out, along with fourteen loaded coal cars. That afternoon a canal boat washed out of the C&O canal and took out another span. That evening half the wyed-span trestle washed out, carrying away twelve loaded coal cars.[12] Crews rebuilt the river trestle by May 4, 1862, but just one month later, on June 7, another flood carried off the entire structure. Workmen rebuilt it and the line reopened on June 15, 1862.[13]

By mid-1862 the railroad was exasperated, and decided to replace the entire bridge with iron Bollman spans. This required adding 5 feet to the tops of the piers, both to accept the new end towers and for better protection from floodwaters. The spans at mid-river were the most difficult to re-trestle, thus they were replaced first. On June 24, 1862, bridge crews under the direction of Wendel Bollman himself began erecting a Bollman truss on span four, completing it and span three by mid-August.[14] Preparations were made to erect span five, but it was not completed.[15]

In September, 1862, the rebels returned during the Antietam campaign and again laid waste to the railroad. Confederate troops destroyed much of the B&O main stem between Harpers Ferry and Martinsburg and absconded with equip-

*Figure 6-The partially rebuilt bridge was again destroyed during the Antietam campaign in September 1862. Here a temporary line is already in place. (NPS photo.)*

*Figure 7-The B&O's bridge near the war's end, with Bollman trusses at mid-river and temporary trestlework at both ends. (NPS photo.)*

ment, using teams of horses to haul locomotives over dirt roads into southern territory. They blew up the two new Bollman trusses (spans three and four) as well as Bollman's original 1852 Winchester span. Troops also burned the remainder of the temporary Potomac trestle, twenty-four spans of armory-trestle woodwork, the boatway trestle, and the 148-foot-long government power canal bridge. The latter had been the last undamaged wooden bridge remaining between Monocacy and Cumberland.[16]

When repair crews returned on September 24, 1862, they faced a desolate scene. The charred remains of locomotives and rolling stock lay everywhere, in some cases thrown off the tracks and into the river or the C&O Canal. One locomotive dangled in the trestlework at the west end of the Potomac bridge, while another sat burned in the tunnel west of town.[17] Still, the line reopened by October 2, 1862.

Meanwhile, other crews were in the river salvaging iron from the demolished Bollman spans. The salvaged iron was used to replace the trestlework at span

five with a Bollman truss.[18] Work began on erecting a Bollman truss for span six on February 9, 1863, and it was finished in just five days, on February 14. Span four was replaced by a Bollman between March 11 and March 18, while work on the Bollman across span three began on April 13, and was finished on April 22.[19] At this time the mid-river spans were Bollmans, while the canal span and the last two western spans (the wyed span plus both arms of the Y) were still trestlework.[20] These central Bollman spans, though sustaining superficial damage at various times, survived the war and would stand until 1936.

*Figure 8-Methods of railroad destruction and repair were refined to an art in the Civil War. Railroad crews regularly performed Herculean tasks to keep the B&O main stem open at Harpers Ferry. On the heels of battle, repair crews would go to work under the guard of an armored train. Often, the railroad used small prefabricated spans for temporary repairs, such as this 50-foot-long, wood- and wrought-iron Bollman deck truss, which could be quickly hoisted into place between trestle bents. (IHTIA, drawing by author.)*

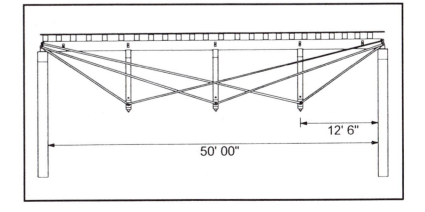

*Figure 9-A photo taken on July 5, 1863, during the Confederate retreat from Gettysburg, showing the Bollman spans with their wood flooring on fire. This view is from the Maryland shore, with the main stem and turnpike in the foreground. (NPS photo.)*

Southern troops retreating from Gettysburg passed through town on July 5, 1863. They laid wood flooring across the spans for their troops and wagons to use, prompting Union cavalry under General Henry A. Cole to raid the town and burn the woodwork on the four Bollman spans and the C&O canal trestle. The line was reopened by July 22, 1863.[21]

On April 10, 1864, the wyed-span, Winchester-span, and curved-span trestlework washed out in a flood along with twelve loaded coal cars and was not repaired until April 18. Workers bridged the gap temporarily with a cable suspension bridge between the intact mid-river spans and the west abutment, and the company transferred passengers, freight, and troops across this span by foot.[22] On May 16, 1864, the water rose again and carried off the government pontoon bridge, and many of the pontoon bridge's floats wedged up against the Potomac trestle. Later that day the floodwaters carried away the wyed-span, Winchester-span, and curved-span trestle (except six bents at the west shore), along with fourteen loaded coal cars. Once the water receded on May 19, it took only two days to replace the trestle.[23]

On July 2, 1864, during Jubal Early's abortive raid into the North, the Confederates again passed through Harpers Ferry. As a precaution Union troops retreated across the bridge to the Maryland side, burning the trestlework at the bridge's west end, and removed the pontoon bridge. On July 6, 1864, the rebels burned the C&O canal trestle, the woodwork on the Bollman spans, and "the timber, track and platforms" on sixteen spans of the armory trestle, all of which work crews repaired by mid-July.[24]

This marked the end of serious fighting at Harpers Ferry. After July, 1864, the various bridges and trestles in town survived unscathed through the war's end in the spring of 1865. But repair work was never finished, and on May 22, 1865, just over a month after Lincoln's assassination, the river rose again and took out the trestlework of the Winchester and wyedspan. Repair crews replaced both by May 27, 1865.[25]

The war forever changed the face of Harpers Ferry, and the town began to fade as an industrial center. Many of the town's homes and business were destroyed, including the armory and arsenal, and were never rebuilt. However, the B&O's far-flung business empire possessed resources which even war could not overcome, and the railroad fully recovered. The loss of the original Latrobe/Wernwag bridge, while disastrous for the B&O in the short term, was probably a more poetic end for the historic span than its inevitable alternative. The increasing tonnage carried by the railroad, especially coal, meant that most of the main stem's wooden spans were reaching the point where they needed replacement. Being one of the oldest wooden bridges on the line at the war's outset meant the B&O probably would have replaced the Harpers Ferry bridge with Bollman trusses during the 1860s anyway.

## Post-War Rebuilding/1868-1894

After the war, the B&O began rebuilding the line at Harpers Ferry in a more permanent manner. In 1866, the B&O replaced the trestle across the government power canal, upriver from the armory grounds, with a 156-foot-long, skewed, double-track Bollman truss.[26] It sat at a 43-degree angle to the canal. Both the

*Figure 10-The government power canal bridge erected in 1866; photo ca. 1880. (NPS photo.)*

boatway and tilt hammer bridges were rebuilt with Bollman deck trusses.

The B&O erected the remaining Bollman spans on the Potomac bridge in 1868, maintaining the span lengths from the Latrobe/Wernwag bridge. Before erecting spans 6 and 7, the company rebuilt pier F (the towpath pier) and the east abutment using granite, not the Tomstown Formation limestone used in the original piers. The new towpath pier was rectangular, and smaller than its predecessor. Two low wingwalls were built along the shore to support the towpath and pier. It is not clear if the trusses were fabricated by the B&O or by Bollman's Patapsco Bridge Company (or both), and why it took so long to complete the bridge. Visually, the new bridge's superstructure still reflected elements of the Latrobe/Wernwag bridge, and the wyed span still dominated the crossing. Similar to the earlier bridge, the Bollman bridge consisted of three parallel lines of trusses, providing both railroad and highway lanes. The roadway crossing and the junction with the W&P remained on the wyed span. Yet, while the pre-war

Winchester span had only eight panels, the new trusses had ten panels, a modification which strengthened the bridge.

After completion, the B&O's bridge was the most elaborate example of a Bollman truss in existence. It merited mentioning in Bollman's 1884 obituary, "The iron bridge at Harpers Ferry...is Mr. Bollman's master-piece, and is a marvel of skill and beauty. It is the only bridge of the kind in its construction and formation

*Figure 11-A closeup showing the wyed span prior to reconstruction in 1868. (NPS photo.)*

*Figure 12-A ca. 1875 view of the Bollman bridge from the base of Maryland Heights. (NPS photo.)*

known, being the wonder and admiration of American and English engineers...."[27] The intricate webs of iron stretching across the spans mimicked the Victorian architectural style of the late nineteenth century. The B&O's colorful paint scheme for its Bollman bridges added to the effect. Historian Robert Vogel deduced that the color scheme applied to Bollman trusses during the 1870s was deep red for the body of the bridge; deep ivory for the main diagonals, the diagonals within each panel, and parts of the abutment towers and tower caps; and white for the remainder of each abutment

*Figure 13-A schematic of the post-Civil War Bollman bridge. Not to scale. (IHTIA, drawing by author.)*

tower cap. While the paint helped protect the iron:

> Whether or not it was the intention, the composition is not only one of considerable impact, but a graphic statement of the structure's functionality as well. The tensile and compressive elements of the truss are dramatically separated: the former light and airy; the latter dark and heavy; a rational reflection of their respective structural roles.[28]

Bollman trusses painted in such striking colors were a breathtaking sight, but over the years the bridge's beauty slowly faded. The B&O reinforced parts of the

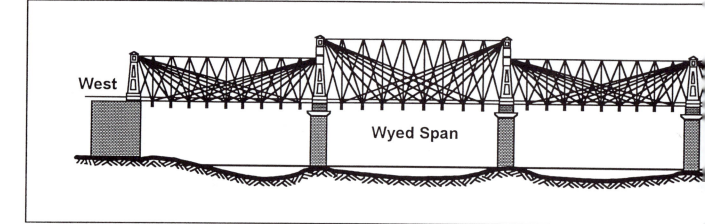

West

Wyed Span

bridge (and the trestle along the armory) with timbers and bracing as the weight of locomotives and rolling stock increased. A description by B&O civil engineer William Sisson in 1894 reflected the railroad's situation in Harpers Ferry:

> Owing to wooden reinforcing trusses, additional bracing, etc., having been put in to strengthen the original part of the bridge, it is now quite a complicated-looking affair, and its present condition mainly necessitated the change at Harpers's Ferry. The old main line then follows the

south bank of the Potomac on an iron trestle, reinforced by intermediate wooden bents, for a distance of nearly one-half mile, and, crossing over the old Government canal on a double-track Bollman bridge of 160-ft. span to the foot of the bluffs near Island Park, follows along the West Virginia shore for nearly two miles, at which point it leaves the river.[29]

The condition of the old Bollman bridge and armory trestle, and the serpentine alignment through the area, finally forced the railroad into action. Starting in

*Figure 14-A ca. 1885 view showing the Bollman Bridge and the iron trestle behind the ruins of the armory. The Shenandoah River highway bridge, at right, was destroyed in the 1889 flood. (NPS photo.)*

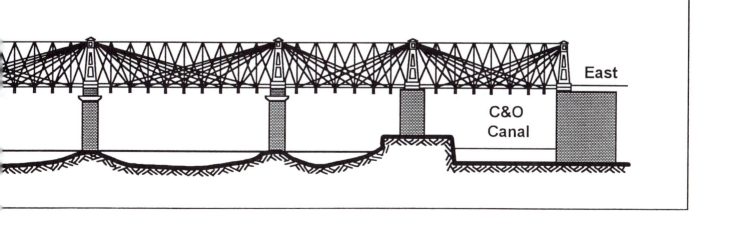

1892, the B&O undertook a number of major improvements at Harpers Ferry, the first substantial changes in the B&O's layout since its arrival nearly sixty years before.

## Notes

1. Anonymous, "Artists' Excursion on The Baltimore and Ohio Railroad," 9.

2. Stinson, "The First Railroad Bridge at Harpers Ferry," 23.

3. Ibid., 24.

4. Ibid., 25.

5. Anonymous Harpers Ferry resident, as quoted in Stinson, 26.

6. David Hunter Strother (Porte Crayon), as quoted in Stinson, 27.

7. Harwood, *Impossible Challenge*, 76.

8. Ibid.

9. Ibid., 77.

10. Ibid.

11. Ibid.

12. Ibid., 78.

13. Ibid.

14. *Baltimore and Ohio Railroad Thirty-Sixth Annual Report, 1862*, 55.

15. Harwood, 78.

16. Ibid.

17. Ibid.

18. *Baltimore and Ohio Railroad Thirty-Seventh Annual Report, 1862*, 43.

19. Harwood, 80-81.

20. Ibid., 84.

21. Ibid.

22. Ibid., 85.

23. Ibid., 87.

24. Ibid.

25. Ibid., 90.

26. Baltimore and Ohio Railroad, Drawing 20095, "Bridge 44," ca. 1918.

27. Anonymous, "The Late Wendel Bollman," 200.

28. Vogel, "Speculations on the History and Original Appearance of the Last Bollman Truss," 436.

29. Sisson, "Harpers Ferry Improvement," 352.

# PART FIVE:

# The 1894 Improvements

## The New Plan

Train operations had never been easy at Harpers Ferry, and the increasing size, length, and weight of trains compounded the problems at the Potomac crossing. Finally, in 1892, during the term of B&O president Charles F. Mayer, the railroad began a project to ease the traffic problems through the section from Sandy Hook, nearly a mile east of Harpers Ferry, to the line's exit from the Potomac Valley upriver from town at Elk Run. The government's abandonment of the armory grounds after the Civil War made the realignment in lower Harpers Ferry possible. "Colonel" James L. Randolph, formerly a chief engineer for the railroad, originally proposed the changes, probably during the 1870s.[1] B&O engineer William Lee Sisson prepared all the plans, except for the bridge superstructure, and supervised the 2-mile rebuild.

The plan dramatically reduced the curvature and gradient through this section by relocating the main stem, boring a 815-foot-long, double-track tunnel through Maryland Heights, and replacing the old Bollman bridge with a modern, double-track bridge on a better alignment. The B&O also rebuilt a section of the old W&P's line (now the B&O's Valley Branch) to allow a better junction with the main stem. The railroad finished the new layout in 1894.

## Grade Relocation

With the armory grounds no longer an obstacle, the B&O abandoned its original alignment along the river wall. This eliminated the need for the iron armory trestle which had served the railroad since the mid-1850s. The wood floor, rails, ties, and the boatway and tilthammer bridges were removed, but the trestle's iron frame-work remained for a few years. Relocation also isolated the power canal bridge, but it and a portion of the old main stem remained in place, used as an industrial siding. This siding served a pulp mill on the armory grounds.

Starting just west of the government power canal span, construction crews cut a new grade into the mountainside (the railroad "daylighted" the short tunnel built through these bluffs in 1840, creating an open cut). The hillside cuts, some of which were 80 feet deep, produced nearly 50,000 cubic yards of rubble. It was used for a new 15-foot-high embankment across the armory grounds, and "the rock, limestone and mica schist, when broken up and hauled an average of 2,600 ft. to [the] embankment, made nearly 90,000 cubic yards, an increase of 80 per cent [over the original volume]."[2] Workers used material from the tunnel excavation through Maryland Heights in a similar manner. The relocated grade curved 9 degrees on the approach embankment. The new bridge sat 8 feet higher at the east end and 11 feet higher at the west end than the old bridge, making it less vulnerable to floods while providing a better gradient. On the

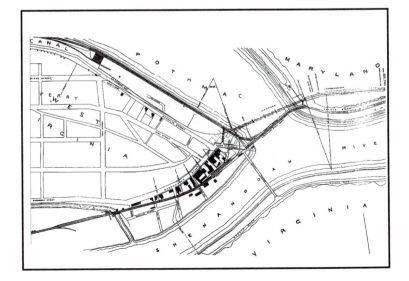

*Figure 1-A map of the 1894 improvements, which included grade relocations on both the B&O and the Valley Branch (formerly the W&P) made possible by the new bridge and tunnel. (From Sisson, "Harpers Ferry Improvement," Plate XLV.)*

*Figure 2-An 1894 photo look-*
*ing up the Potomac Valley*
*shows the new alignment*
*across the armory grounds.*
*Although abandoned, the ar-*
*mory trestle is still in place.*
*(NPS photo.)*

Maryland, or east, shore of the Potomac the line followed a 7 degree curve for 100 feet, entered the new tunnel (see below), and returned to a tangent. This finally removed what had been one of the tightest turns on a main line railroad in the United States. From the tunnel's east end to Sandy Hook (1 mile east of Harpers Ferry), the relocated line sat higher on the riverbank above the C&O Canal, which allowed for a gentle curve back to the original main stem at Sandy Hook.[3]

The new embankment necessitated removal of four Civil War-era structures at the west end of the bridge. Notable among these structures was "John Brown's Fort," the old armory fire-engine house made famous in the 1859 raid. It was dismantled and sent to Chicago for the 1893 Colombian Exposition, and later returned to Harpers Ferry.

Because the embankment across the old armory grounds blocked drainage of water from the downtown (previously it flowed through the boatway), the B&O constructed a masonry, arched drainage culvert from the east end of Shenandoah Street, through the embankment and the 1840 wingwall/causeway, exiting just downstream from the old boatway gap.

The culvert has 5-foot-tall bench walls; the arch a 5-foot radius. Overall, it runs 186 feet east to west, inclined with a grade of 1 foot in 100 for drainage purposes. The Shenandoah Street entrance to this culvert can be easily seen today.

## The New Harpers Ferry Tunnel

From the B&O's arrival at Harpers Ferry in 1834, the railroad was plagued by the lack of space at the foot of Maryland Heights. It was equally confining around the base of the bluff where the county road (the old turnpike), the railroad, and the canal ran side-by-side. To improve the approach to the new bridge the B&O bored an 815-foot-long, double-track tunnel through the granite of Maryland Heights during 1893. It sat on a nearly east-west axis, but had a slight curve at its west end.

The 300 feet of vertical rock face immediately above the tunnel's west portal prevented a standard survey across the top of the mountain to align the tunnel, so the engineers used triangulation. Survey lines were run around the base of the mountain "from which angles and distances were carefully measured...to a point on the center line [of the tunnel] on the east side. The distance measured through the tunnel afterwards was 0.2 of a foot less than that calculated."[4] Workers bored through the hard granite and quartz from both ends of tunnel with Ingersoll-Sergeant pneumatic drills. A steam-powered air compressor at the tunnel's east end supplied the drills. Crews laid pipes around the foot of the mountain to supply compressed air to the drills advancing from the west end.[5] The workers began by excavating the "heading," an arched bore 8 feet high by 25 feet wide, which would later form the arched top section of the tunnel. Other crews excavated the "bench," or the lower section of the tunnel, 15 feet behind the drills advancing at the heading's face. At the east end workers advanced 18 feet per week, equivalent to the removal of 1,604 cubic yards each month. Workers at the west end advanced 19 feet per week, removing 1,692 cubic yards of spoil each month. Spoil was removed and put through a Gates' Company rock crusher at each end of the tunnel.[35] The total amount of rock excavated from the tunnel and both approach cuts was 43,211 cubic yards, which cost $65,265 to remove and crush in preparation for use in the embankment and elsewhere.[6]

The rock was stable enough to support itself during excavation. After completing the bore, workers lined 80 feet at the west end and 45 feet at the east end with limestone masonry sidewalls and a brick-arch roof. Masons built the arch "of five rings of bricks, with benchwalls [sidewalls] of first class stone masonry 2 ft. thick, backed with rubble masonry carried up to a point 9 ft. above the springing line, the remainder of packing being stone placed by hand."[7] The total cost for masonry in the tunnel was $9,874. Using 164 cubic yards of stone, the company constructed limestone portals at both ends for $1,640. Trains bringing structural members to the new bridge site passed through the bore a number of times before workers undertook the arching.[8]

The deep approach cuts at either end of the tunnel caused problems immediately. Aside from the difficulty and cost of excavating them, rock falls immediately rained down from the cliffs, blocking the tracks and threatening employees. To remedy this the company quickly extended the lining of the tunnel about 36 feet on each end and added sufficient covering over the arch to protect it from falling rocks. This lengthened the tunnel to

*Figure 3-After rock falls forced extension of the tunnel lining, brick portals were built in 1896. (NPS photo.)*

*Figure 4-The Shenandoah Street culvert. (IHTIA, photo by author.)*

885 feet. The B&O constructed new brick portals at both ends soon after.[9]

## The 1894 Bridge and the Rise of the Modern Bridge-Building Industry

The centerpiece of the improvements was a new, steel, double-track bridge over the Potomac. It was located on a better alignment and designed to handle much heavier loads than the Bollman bridge. The new tunnel through Maryland Heights eliminated the tight turn once required at the east end of the old bridge. Still, the west end of the 1894 bridge resembled Latrobe's design of sixty years earlier, but it incorporated a better junction to the Valley Branch. This bridge now carries trains from the CSX Valley Branch, and is apparently the oldest through truss in use along the original main stem.

Other changes in the design philosophy between Latrobe in 1836, Bollman in 1852, and the B&O's engineers in 1894, reflect broader trends in the bridge-building industry. The planning, design, and

erection of bridges--like nearly all aspects of railroad construction--underwent major changes during this perod. Widespread usage of iron, the rise of bridge-building companies, the advent of specifications, standardization, materials testing, more accurate theoretical analysis, and the eventual incorporation of steel as a bridge-building material, combined to dramatically change American bridge building.

The years from 1840 to 1880 have been called the golden era of the iron bridge.[10] After the first tentative use of iron components on wooden bridges by engineers like Wernwag and Latrobe, then the full fledged use of iron by Bollman, the iron bridge-truss reached maturity and found common usage across the country. Combinations of cast and wrought iron reached their apex in the railroad crossings over the Ohio and Mississippi Rivers during and just after the Civil War, where single spans reached up to 500 feet in length. Thereafter, bridge companies developed a wide array of cast- and wrought-iron truss arrangements. Smaller iron bridges also became popular throughout the country for use on highways.

One notable aspect of the second half of the century was the rise of bridge-building companies such as W. Bollman & Company--Bollman's own bridge fabricating company formed in 1858 and renamed the Patapsco Bridge and Iron Works after the war.[11] The B&O, like other railroads, generally contracted bridge fabrication out to other companies. Often these companies specialized in building the presiding engineer's patented bridge design, and used standardized "off the shelf" structural members to erect bridges faster and cheaper than ever before. There were only fifteen bridge-building companies active in the United States in 1850, increasing to more than 190 by 1900.[12] That

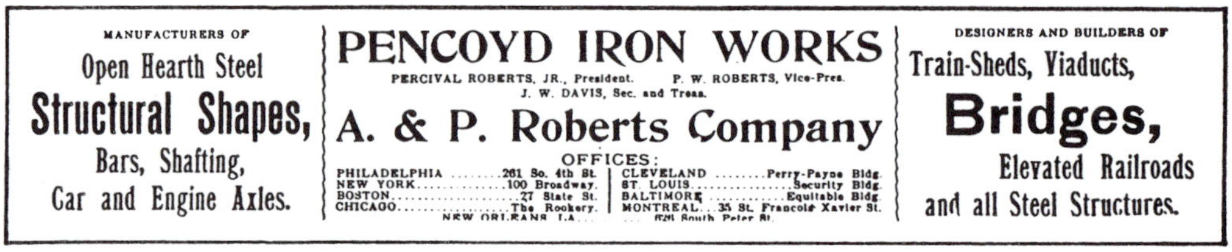

*Figure 5-There were scores of bridge companies in the late 1800s. The Pencoyd Iron Works fabricated and erected the B&O's 1894 bridge. (From **Engineering News**, June 27, 1895, p. 27)*

year, J. P. Morgan's newly formed American Bridge Company (which soon after became a subsidiary of United States Steel Corporation) began consolidation of the industry by purchasing twenty-four companies, representing 50 percent of the nation's bridge fabricating capacity.[13]

The engineer's role also changed in the second half of the nineteenth century. Bridge design was probably the first area of specialization in the field of structural engineering. Beginning in the 1870s, the idiosyncrasies of individual engineers and bridge-building companies began fading out as the use of standardized rolled-steel shapes, performance specifications, more accurate rolling-load analysis, and materials testing became commonplace. To a large extent, the influence of individual personalities (such as Bollman or Latrobe) was lost as projects were divided among large staffs of engineers with little leeway for personal experimentation, and the heroic age of bridge engineering faded. Bridge-building companies remained viable, but their engineers gradually accepted a more homogenous design philosophy.

Perhaps the most monumental change was the adoption of steel for bridge building in the last two decades of the 1800s. With the increasing use of the Bessemer and open hearth steel-making processes (which for the first time produced comparatively low-cost, high-quality, high-strength steel and steel alloys in large quantities) cast and wrought iron passed out of use as a structural component by the 1890s. Extensive use of steel began about 1880, only being used in isolated cases before this, such as James Eads' crossing of the Mississippi River at St. Louis in 1874.

A primary reason for the fading of cast- and wrought-iron truss arrangements was that engineers found them generally deficient under the increasing loads they were expected to carry. Cast iron is brittle and could fail without warning. In addition, the quality of early cast iron varied, and castings often had inclusions such as

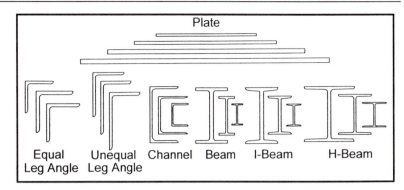

air bubbles and internal flaws. Widely reported disasters such as the Ashtabula (Ohio) bridge collapse, which killed ninety-two persons in 1876, led to a general mistrust of cast-iron bridge components. In 1889, noted bridge engineer Theodore Cooper commented that, "The old forms [in cast and wrought iron], like the Bollman, Fink, Lowthorp and Post trusses, have disappeared from American practice."[14] By 1894 engineers found it nearly impossible to obtain cast iron in structural forms, although it was still used for certain low-risk components such as bearing plates. Thus, the combination of increasing train weights, mistrust of early cast-iron bridge components, and the advent of steel culminated in the replacement of thousands of cast- and wrought-iron bridges across the country in the 1890s with new steel bridges.

During the same period, civil engineers generally stopped constructing through trusses for railroad spans less than 80 feet long, instead opting for girders made of riveted steel plates, or rolled beams for very short spans (these are discussed in detail in Part Six). The overall form, or silhouette, of trusses also began to change--growing taller, often incorporating camelback top chords, inclined end posts, and built-up latticework beams--further increasing economy and possible span lengths. During this period, two older truss layouts, the Pratt truss and Warren truss, became immensely popular with engineers. In the B&O's case, as its Bollman and Fink trusses grew obsolete in the 1880s and 1890s, the company began favoring Pratt-type trusses. Later (in the early twentieth century) the B&O

*Figure 6-Cross sections of common rolled-steel structural shapes used in bridge construction in the latter half of the nineteenth century. These could be used individually or combined to create larger members. (IHTIA, drawing by author.)*

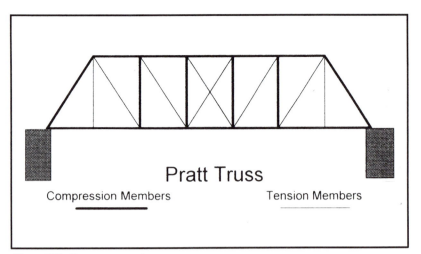

Pratt Truss

Compression Members                    Tension Members

*Figure 7-The Pratt truss, a main-stay for bridge designers every-where. (IHTIA, drawing by author.)*

switched to Warren trusses. While these latter truss layouts were perfected by rail-roads, they worked equally well for high-way bridges.

The Pratt truss originated as a wood and iron truss patented in 1844 by Thomas and Caleb Pratt. It consisted of wooden vertical members acting in com-pression and wrought-iron diagonals act-ing in tension, which minimizes the length of the compression members and re-duces their tendency to buckle under load. Soon, cast and wrought-iron Pratt trusses became popular among engineers, and im-provements to the truss layout allowed longer, stronger spans. Squire Whipple in-troduced the *double-intersection* form of the Pratt truss, which overlapped two inde-pendent systems of Pratt trusses and al-lowed for longer spans. This form was also known either as the Whipple, Whip-ple-Murphy, or Linville truss--and it found extensive use after the Civil War un-til the turn of the century.[15] Other new truss designs, including the Baltimore (or Petit) truss, the Pennsylvania truss, and the Kellogg truss, all derivatives of the Pratt truss, were also popularized during this time but have since faded from use. These more complicated truss arrange-ments arose because the length of deck chords on Pratt trusses reached the point where the deck needed secondary support to prevent excessive deflection.

Bridge superstructures were also changing in another way. From the 1850s

to the turn of the century, the pin-con-nected joint, as opposed to the riveted joint, was preferred for primary structural members because it was easier to calcu-late stresses at work in the truss, and was easier and faster to erect with semi-skilled labor. Bollman trusses were an early ex-ample of this, using large wrought-iron pins to connect suspension bars to each abutment tower. Pin-connected steel bridge trusses became standard in Amer-ica, and Pratt and Warren trusses re-mained the most popular layouts. Begin-ning in the 1890s, the riveted connection gained favor because of its increased stiff-ness, which meant less counter bracing, and developments which made riveting quicker and more reliable.[16] Nonetheless, the Pratt and Warren layouts predomi-nated, and most other truss forms faded from use. The advent of steel and the drive toward standardization and economy helped ensure their use throughout the twentieth century.

The nine steel spans of the 1894 Poto-mac bridge superstructure are a combina-tion of three Pratt through trusses and six deck plate-girder spans, representing the state of the bridge-building art as prac-ticed on the B&O in 1894. Though not a particularly long or massive bridge for the period, it is an excellent representative of steel, pin-connected trusses and stand-ardized bridge design at the turn of the century.

## New Abutments and Piers

New abutments were built on both sides of the Potomac just upstream from the old bridge. The new west abutment protruded from the 1842 wingwall, but otherwise the improvements left the La-trobe/Wernwag bridge masonry intact. The company constructed eight new piers to carry the bridge across the Potomac, lo-cating them directly upstream of the old bridge piers to obstruct the overall flow of water as little as possible. The piers were set on a 73-degree angle to the center line of the bridge superstructure. Cofferdams protected the construction crews sinking the foundations from the 6-foot-deep

water. For the cofferdams, crews used "Wakefield sheet piling," an early system of interlocking steel piles. The uneven bedrock in the riverbed required rough sections to be cut away. Workers excavated some 2,406 cubic yards of material from the riverbed in sinking the foundations for the piers, using the rubble for the armory embankment fill.[17]

Crews poured concrete foundations consisting of one part Portland cement, two parts river sand, and five parts broken stone to form a level base for the masonry.[18] The piers and new abutments required 3,552 cubic yards of rock-faced, random ashlar masonry, 1,404 cubic yards of rubble masonry, 340 cubic yards of concrete, and 4,068 barrels of cement, which cost the B&O $49,910. Each pier is constructed of local "Gettysburg Granite" founded on solid rock, tapering to 6 feet wide by 37 feet long on top.[19]

## Bridge Superstructure

While the B&O attempted to alleviate the problems caused by the old wyed span, the mid-river junction still survived on the 1894 bridge in a new form. The junction remained over the river, but now the Valley Branch line had to curve to meet it, leaving the main stem's section of the bridge on a tangent, which was the opposite of Latrobe's compromise in 1836. More importantly, the old turnpike was no longer on the bridge and the B&O finally had a double-track crossing (the Bollman span became solely a highway bridge).

Pencoyd Bridge and Construction Company of Philadelphia, which later be-

came part of the American Bridge Company, fabricated the superstructure's steelwork in 1893 and carried out its erection during the next year. Mild steel formed the Pratt trusses, except for the eye-bars, pins, and rollers which were formed from medium steel. The inclined end posts and top and bottom chords are riveted box girders with open latticework bottoms. The vertical (compression) members are large twin channel beams connected with riveted latticework. Forged eyebars form the diagonals (tension members) on the end panels, while the hip verticals and the center panels' diagonals are heavier latticed beams to compensate for secondary stresses.[20] Likewise, the struts across the top of bridge, portal, and portal bracing are angle bars connected by riveted latticework. A Pencoyd Company builder's plate is riveted to the downstream inclined endpost at the west portal. The bridge's other six spans (seven counting the Valley Branch span) are riveted steel-plate deck girders, with each span made up of three parallel girders spaced 9 feet apart. At mid-river the bridge deck is 40 feet above the river bottom. Engineers designed the bridge for a moving load on each track of two 125-ton Consolidation locomotives coupled together, followed by a train load of 4,000 pounds per linear foot as required by Theodore Cooper's specifications (the industry standard at the time).[21]

*Figure 8-The westernmost Pratt truss on the 1894 bridge. The end posts are inclined at slightly different angles to compensate for the skew of the bridge, allowing the various cross struts to connect perpendicularly to the top and bottom chords. (IHTIA, photo by author.)*

*Figure 9-Measurements of the 1894 bridge superstructure, east to west. (Sisson, "Harpers Ferry Improvement," p. 355.)*

| Span Number/ Comments | Span Type | Vertical Dimension (or depth) | Truss Length (center to center of piers) |
|---|---|---|---|
| #1/over county road | Deck Girder | App. 4' | 33' 3" |
| #2/over C&O Canal | Deck Girder | 7' 10" | 100' |
| #3 | Deck Girder | 7' 10" | 85' 6" |
| #4 | Pratt Through Truss | 30' | 140' |
| #5 | Pratt Through Truss | 30' | 140' |
| #6 | Pratt Through Truss | 30' | 140' |
| #7 | Deck Girder | 7' 10" | 85' 6" |
| #8/mimics old wyed span | Deck Girder | 7' 10" | 85' 6" |
| #9 | Deck Girder | 7' 10" | 90' 7" |
| #9B/Valley Branch connection, single-track | Deck Girder | 7' 10" | 64' 3" |

*Figure 10-A vertical latticed beam on the 1894 Pratt truss. (IHTIA, photo by author.)*

A wood floor was built between the two arms of the wye for a passenger platform, and iron fencing erected along the deck spans to protect passengers. For unknown reasons, in 1911 the B&O replaced span number one (a deck girder) with a span fabricated by the American Bridge Company.

### The 1894 Depot

Following the Civil War a three-story tavern and hotel served as the depot until 1894, and "the passenger platform was on the trestle behind the building at the second-floor level."[22] A wood-frame building between the old W&P and the main stem, built after the war, remained as a carpenter's shop. However, after demolishing the hotel building and creating the embankment, the railroad needed a new depot. During 1894, as the new bridge

*Figure 11-A plan view (above) and schematic elevation (below) of the 1894 Pencoyd Company Bridge. Schematic not to scale. (Baltimore and Ohio Railroad, Drawing, 4964, "Harpers Ferry," 1950; and IHTIA, drawing by author.)*

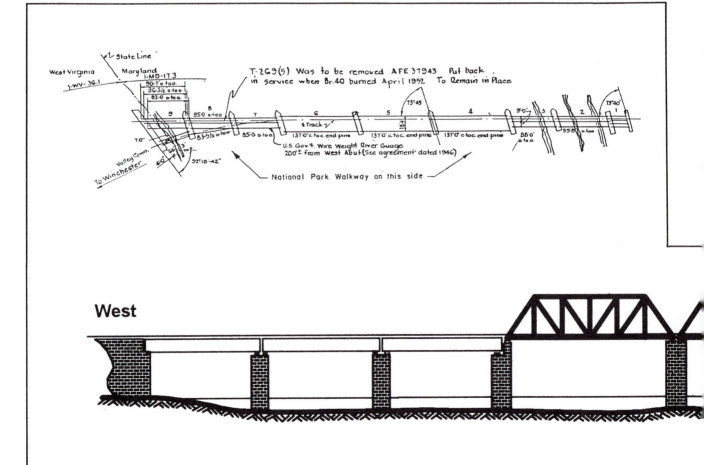

neared completion, the railroad erected a Francis Baldwin-designed depot on the embankment at the west end of the bridge. During the 1880s and 1890s the B&O employed Baldwin, a prominent Baltimore architect, to produce a number of depot designs for its lines. The Harpers Ferry depot apparently was unique among these. It was a 25-foot by 120-foot, wood-frame, combination passenger and freight depot. Except for an ornate, Victorian-style, two-story interlocking tower at the east end (which held the switching apparatus for the Valley Branch junction), it was a single-story building. The company built a small passenger shelter on the other side of the tracks, opposite the depot's telegrapher bay. The shelter was rebuilt and given a walkway underpass to the depot in 1911, providing safer passenger transferrals.[23] The passenger platform around the depot extended over the space between the arms of the Y at the west end of the new bridge. This depot served both the main stem and Valley Branch.

## Elk Run Culvert

The 1894 improvements extended up the Potomac from Harpers Ferry, and this may have been when the B&O built a picturesque, horseshoe-shaped culvert across Elk Run. This 17-foot-wide masonry arch exhibits beautiful stonework, but why such attention for a lowly culvert? During the 1890s, the B&O operated an amusement park nearby on an island in

*Figure 12-A ca. 1900 photo of the Francis Baldwin-designed depot. (NPS photo.)*

the Potomac reached by a footbridge from trackside. This culvert was also within view of a public road (dating from before the Civil War)--thus the aesthetic treatment. However, the culvert may date to much earlier, possibly the main stem's original construction in 1840-42. Its neo-Egyptian flavor suggests the influence of Benjamin Latrobe Jr., who had a fondness for this style.

Overall, the 1894 improvements dramatically changed the appearance of Harpers Ferry and gave it the current street layout. Today, the 1894 bridge and embankment are the most prominant railroad

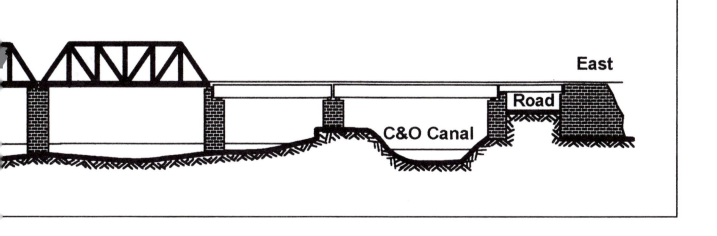

*Figure 13-Elk Run culvert in 1997. (IHTIA, photo by author.)*

features visible to visitors of the lower town. The original site of John Brown's Fort is marked by an obelisk atop the embankment, near the corner of Potomac and Shenandoah Streets.

## Notes

1.  Sisson, "Harpers Ferry Improvement," 354.

2.  Ibid., 352.

3.  Ibid., 354.

4.  Ibid., 355.

5.  Ibid., 354.

6.  Ibid.

7.  Ibid.

8.  Ibid.

9.  National Archive Record Group 134, Interstate Commerce Commission Railroad Valuation Records, Structure Notes, B&O Railroad, Maintenance of Way Department Tunnel Report, ca. 1918, 7.

10. DeLony, "The Golden Age of the Iron Bridge," 8.

11. Darnell, *A Directory of American Bridge-Building Companies: 1840-1900*, vii.

12. DeLony, 20.

13. Darnell, 85.

14. Cooper, "American Railroad Bridges," 48.

15. Weitzman, *Traces to the Past*, 104.

16. Ibid., 80.

17. Sisson, 354.

18. Ibid.

19. Ibid., 355.

20. Ibid.

21. Ibid.

22. Harwood, *Impossible Challenge*, 127.

23. Anonymous, "Subways for Safety," 10.

# PART SIX:

# The 1931 Improvements, the Main Stem Today, and Final Thoughts

*Figure 1-This June 9, 1931, photo shows the final layout at the Potomac crossing. The depot has been relocated and the new tunnel portal completed, and the new bridge is in use. For five years, three periods in the history of bridge engineering were represented side by side. (NPS photo.)*

## The 1931 Improvements

The 1894 bridge served its purpose well for thirty-five years, but by 1930 the Baltimore and Ohio planned another round of improvements at Harpers Ferry. This was carried out during the term of the B&O's longest serving president, Daniel Willard, who led the company from 1910 to 1941. By this time the B&O's engineer of bridges was Philip G. Lang Jr., who served in this position from 1921 to around 1945, and he probably planned and oversaw the project.[1] Again, the railroad needed a stronger bridge, but more importantly another grade realignment would finally eliminate the need for a bridge junction by using the 1894 bridge to carry the Valley Branch traffic. The

new bridge, just up the Potomac from the 1894 bridge, was sharply angled to the river to reduce curvature at both ends and allowed trains to maintain higher speeds through the area. Its superstructure consists entirely of steel-plate girders, the most widely used type of railroad bridge in America today. The B&O also widened the tunnel's west end to nearly 45 feet, removing clearance restrictions in the tunnel by cutting farther into the north side of the approach cut and rebuilding the cut and cover section with a new reinforced-concrete lining and portal. The company moved the Valley Branch junction across the river, to just inside the new tunnel entrance. The 1931 improvements were the railroad's last major alterations to the Potomac crossing. For the next five years, Harpers Ferry possessed a unique collection of railroad bridges representing three distinct periods of bridge-building technology.

## The 1931 Bridge and the Steel-Plate Girder

The new bridge was built during 1930-1931, and it represents the maturation of short- to medium-length steel bridges. From an aesthetic standpoint, it is the least attractive of the various bridges that have spanned the rivers here, but functionally it is superior to its more graceful ancestors. Metal girders and rolled beams have their origins in the earliest cast-iron rails developed in Britain in the late eighteenth century. British and American engineers developed a wide variety of metal plate girders, rolled beams, and hollow box girders during the nineteenth century. By 1845, engineers in Britain, such as Robert Stephenson, had even built monumental "tubular" bridges using giant wrought-iron box girders which trains travelled *through*. Different configurations of the web and top and bottom flanges allowed girders and beams to serve many different purposes in bridge building (they also led to a revolution in general construction, culminating in the modern steel-frame skyscraper). The built-up girder, constructed from numerous individual plates riveted together to the desired depth and length, showed it-

self to be both economical and reliable, essential prerequisites for railroad usage.

James Milholland built the first metal girder bridge in the United States, a 50-foot span for the Baltimore and Susquehanna Railroad at Bolton Station, Maryland, in 1846-47. Yet, until the late 1800s metal girders and beams were more often incorporated as secondary members on bridges (such as the floor beams on Bollman trusses). Still, early forms of plate-girder bridges were very similar to their modern counterparts, usually consisting of two or more parallel girders lying under grade, connected with cross-braces, and the track supported on closely spaced ties resting directly on the top flange (a *deck* girder) or bottom flange (a *through* girder). The advent of structural steel after the Civil War and improvements in rolling and riveting steel forms meant that extremely strong plate girders could be fabricated at a relatively low cost. As shown in the 1894 Potomac bridge, the steel girder had gained wide use by the late nineteenth century. Because ballast improved the ride, railroad girder-bridges were sometimes topped with a concrete deck and layer of ballast to support the ties. Beginning around 1900, steel girders were often totally encased in concrete for added protection and strength.

By the 1930s, bridge engineers preferred steel girders for spans up to 130 feet (or as long as could be carried by flatcars to the site), and they have been used ever since on railroads and highways wherever the situation allowed. Compared to standard through trusses, the steel girder is easier to fabricate, transport, and erect; more durable with less necessary upkeep; safer (a derailment will not damage the superstructure as easily); and stronger in short spans. Where spans could be kept short without obstructing navigation, such as at Harpers Ferry, designers nearly always opted for shorter deck-girder spans instead of longer through-truss spans. Today, deck girders are found everywhere, and most likely will remain the bridge of choice for short- to medium-length spans in the foreseeable future. The vast majority of metal bridges remaining

*Figure 2-Details of a typical deck plate girder. (From Urquhart and O'Rourke, Design of Steel Structures, p. 106.)*

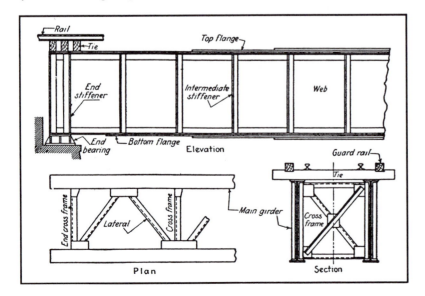

along the functioning sections of the B&O's original main stem are steel girders fabricated between 1900 and 1950. The popularization of diesel locomotives in the 1940s, which reversed the trend toward ever-heavier motive power, means that bridges built with steam locomotives in mind are still more than adequate for modern diesel locomotives.

## New Abutments and Piers

In 1931 the B&O built reinforced-concrete abutments on either side of the river (upstream from the 1894 bridge abutments) and thirteen river piers. The piers and abutments illustrate another change in construction practices from 1894. The development of reinforced concrete after the turn of the century provided a new structural material for engineers to incorporate into bridges. Concrete by itself lacks tensile strength, but the addition of steel bars solved this problem and made it a versatile and strong building material. Thereafter, engineers often used reinforced concrete instead of the more difficult to erect, more labor intensive and expensive stone masonry.

Construction crews sank the foundations for the piers at a time of very low water in the Potomac, and they worked with heavy equipment in the river bed using only minimal cofferdams. Wooden forms were built and steel reinforcing bars placed to await the concrete, which was made on the site. The piers were founded on solid rock (the foundation pads measuring approximately 20 feet wide, 50 feet long, and 5 feet deep) and rose 35 feet

above the foundations. A pedestrian tunnel provided access through the west abutment to a passenger shed across from the depot.[2] When compared to the 1894 bridge's abutment, the west abutment for the 1931 bridge sets considerably farther back from the river on the armory grounds, leaving the armory wall untouched. The new approach to the bridge's west end required another embankment across the armory grounds.

*Figure 4-A 1997 view from the Maryland shore showing the downstream side of the 1931 bridge. The pier at right sits along the C&O Canal towpath. (IHTIA, photo by author.)*

## The Superstructure

The superstructure consists of fourteen deck-girder spans. It is 1,362 feet long, averaging approximately 47 feet from the riverbed to the top of the rails, and crosses the Potomac River at a much sharper angle than its predecessors.

The American Bridge Company fabricated the girders, and they were brought to the site on flatcars and hoisted into place by a rail-mounted crane.[3] This is a fine example of the standardized, optimized bridge, with little flamboyance or risk in the design. It consists of four lines of parallel girders--one under each rail--totalling roughly 4,400,000 pounds of steel.[4] The rails were carried by closely spaced wooden crossties resting directly on the girders. Wooden walkways with steel handrails and light posts lined the bridge on either side, and another walkway was centered between the tracks.

*Figure 3-A November 1930 photo of the reinforced-concrete piers under construction. (NPS photo)*

| Span Number/ Comments | Span Type | Vertical Dimension or Girder Depth | Girder Length |
|---|---|---|---|
| #1/County Road | Steel Plate Girder | 10' | 67' 7" to 55' 1.5" |
| #2/C&O Canal | Steel Plate Girder | 10' | 100' |
| #3 | Steel Plate Girder | 10' | 100' |
| #4 | Steel Plate Girder | 10' | 100' |
| #5 | Steel Plate Girder | 10' | 100' |
| #6 | Steel Plate Girder | 10' | 100' |
| #7 | Steel Plate Girder | 10' | 100' |
| #8 | Steel Plate Girder | 10' | 100' |
| #9 | Steel Plate Girder | 10' | 100' |
| #10 | Steel Plate Girder | 10' | 100' |
| #11 | Steel Plate Girder | 10' | 100' |
| #12 | Steel Plate Girder | 10' | 100' |
| #13 | Steel Plate Girder | 10' | 100' |
| #14 | Steel Plate Girder | 10' | 100' to 91' 4" |

*Figure 5-Span types and dimensions (east to west) of the 1931 bridge illustrate the railroad's drive towards standardization. Its overall length is 1,362 feet. The girders of the end spans are a variety of lengths because the piers are set at an angle to the abutments. (Baltimore and Ohio Railroad, Drawing 3191, "Bridge 40," 1931.)*

The railroad opened the bridge on June 1, 1931.[5]

After 1931, the 1894 bridge carried only the Valley Branch traffic, and the B&O removed the downstream set of rails. An on-shore connection between the main stem and Shenandoah Valley Branch was later converted to a siding and eventually removed altogether. The National Park Service constructed a walkway across the downstream section of the

bridge and today it carries the Appalachian Trail across the Potomac, a fitting addition to the Harpers Ferry roster of transportation links.

Incredibly, the 1931 bridge's wooden deck and ties were accidentally set on fire three times. The first was on March 6, 1931, prior to the bridge's opening, and may have been caused by welding crews. It caught fire again on April 11th, 1951, when sparks from a steam locomotive ignited the ties. The final occasion was on June 9, 1956, when a coal car derailed on the bridge. Its spilled load somehow caught fire and burned the woodwork.[6] As a consequence, in 1957 the B&O installed firestops on each span to prevent a recurrence of the problem. These are steel "curtains" between the girders across the width of the bridge, under the rails and largely out of sight. The 1931 bridge has continued to serve the B&O, and now CSX, to this day, and should into the foreseeable future.

## Harpers Ferry Depot, 1931-1997

On February 2, 1931, following the alignment change, the B&O moved the 1894 depot to the west end of the new bridge. The station was jacked up, slid onto railroad cars, and carried to the new site. The construction crews then wheeled

*Figure 6-The aftermath of the April 1951 fire. The extreme heat warped the bridge's secondary members. (NPS photo.)*

*Figure 7-A ca. 1900 view looking east through the Bollman bridge. After 1894 the spans carried pedestrians, horse-drawn wagons, and eventually automobiles. (NPS photo.)*

the building the remaining distance to its current position. When the company moved the depot, they also constructed a new, larger passenger shelter across the tracks from the station. Access to the shelter is through a tunnel piercing the west bridge abutment. The Victorian switch/telegraph tower and the ticket bay were removed ca. 1950. This depot has had a long life, though now it barely resembles its original appearance. It is currently used by CSX as a section office and is an active commuter station.

## Removal of the Government Power Canal Bridge

When the company relocated the mainline in 1894, it left part of the line to function as an industrial siding for a pulp mill on the armory grounds near the old tilt hammer bridge. The B&O converted the 1866 Bollman into a single track span in 1894, and strengthened it over the years with wood beams and structural-steel members. It was one of the few surviving Bollman-truss bridges when finally removed in 1933.

## The Bollman Bridge after 1894 and its Destruction in the 1936 Flood

Upon completing the 1894 improvements, the B&O converted the old Bollman bridge to highway use. After remov-

ing the downstream line of trusses and the old curved span (the main stem's leg of the wye), the company took up the rails from the remaining spans and laid flooring for road traffic. Ownership was conveyed to the county soon after decommissioning as a railroad bridge. The bridge remained in this form until 1924, when a flood destroyed the three easternmost Bollman spans. Two Warren-trusses (at spans seven and eight) and a Pratt through-truss span (at span six) replaced the Bollmans. This made the fourth type of truss system placed on the original 1836 piers.

While not associated with the railroad in this particular case, the Warren truss, like the Pratt truss, represents another very successful bridge type. The modern Warren truss began as a wood and iron truss patented in 1848 by James Warren (in the United States) and Theobald Monzani (in Britain). It consists solely of triangular panels, with each diagonal sloping toward the next. There are no vertical members, and the diagonals undergo both compressive and tensile forces. This layout's simplicity was perhaps its greatest strength. Like the Pratt, the Warren truss was reincarnated in cast and wrought iron, and then steel. Like the Pratt, Warren trusses could be subdivided with vertical and diagonal secondary members, but with the incorporation of steel they gravitated toward simple, clean lines. By the 1890s Warren trusses were widely used on American railroads, and the B&O adopted them in the early twentieth cen-

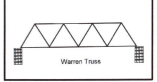

*Figure 8-The Warren truss. Warren and Pratt trusses were the most successful truss types arising from bridge construction in the nineteenth century. (IHTIA, drawing by author.)*

*Figure 9-The west end of the Bollman bridge just prior to collapse in the 1936 flood. (IHTIA, Frank Duff McEnteer Collection.)*

*Figure 10-An aerial view of the Harpers Ferry crossing, ca. 1960. Note the remains of the 1836 bridge piers. (NPS photo.)*

tury. As represented here, they were also popular for highway bridges and remain so to this day.

By the 1930s the once-majestic Bollman bridge had lost much of its former glory; advertising billboards hung off its sides, and it apparently had not received a coat of paint in forty years. The bridge superstructure--four remaining Bollman spans and the replacement highway trusses--finally collapsed in a powerful flood on March 17, 1936. After the waters receded, all that remained of the Bollman bridge was a cast-iron tower on the west abutment--the rest lay strewn in the river. The flood also destroyed piers C and D, leaving only rubble. The remaining Warren truss, span seven, was later removed. In 1997, only the two western-most river piers (A and B) and the tow-path pier remain, along with the abutments on either shore. Parts of the Bollman were recovered by the National Park Service, and will be used to interpret the history of this important bridge.

## Harpers Ferry Today/Where to See the B&O's Remains

Presently, CSX maintains the very active line through Harpers Ferry, and the 1931 and 1894 bridges are still heavily used. Numerous features relating to the B&O's main stem can be easily seen by visitors.

(1) Portions of the main stem's original route abandoned in 1894 are evident on both sides of the Potomac.

(2) The west abutment and two piers of the original Latrobe/Wernwag-designed bridge remain relatively intact. The others are in ruins, washed away in the March 1936 flood and subsequent freshets. On the two remaining piers, the 5-foot additions dating to the Civil War are clearly identifiable. The existing east abutment and towpath pier date to ca. 1866. The square, granite bases of the Bollman truss end towers are still in place on the piers and both abutments (the piers are listed on the National Register of Historic Places). Parts of a Bollman truss recovered from the river by the National Park Service are from the 1868 Winchester span.

(3) The abutment (ca. 1840) of the Latrobe-designed curved span is intact. The upstream wingwall/causeway is intersected by the 1894 bridge abutment and the 1894 drainage culvert.

(4) The 1840 armory and river walls both remain, though the river wall is the only one clearly visible. The gaps left in the wall at the boatway and tilt hammer crossings are visible, as well as a number of drainage openings. The 1931 bridge abutment was built on the armory grounds, leaving the walls untouched.

(5) The abutments of the government power canal span probably date to 1840

*Figure 11-A closeup of pier A, with alterations clearly visible and bases for the Bollman end towers still in place. (IHTIA, photo by author.)*

and are extant. The granite bases for the end towers from the 1866 Bollman truss are in place.

(6) The 1894 depot, although relocated to its current position and altered by the removal of its interlocking tower, remains in use.

(7) The 1894 Potomac bridge, while not nearly as significant as the earlier Latrobe/Wernwag bridge, is nonetheless over one hundred years old (except for one small replacement span dating from 1911), and is the oldest through-truss bridge in use along the B&O's original main stem. The public walkway across this span provides excellent views of the engineering features in and along the river.

(8) Other features of the 1894 improvements, such as the Harpers Ferry tunnel, the embankment through the armory grounds, and the drainage culvert through the embankment at the end of Shenandoah Street, are still maintained by the railroad.

(9) The 1931 Potomac bridge and the "new" Harpers Ferry tunnel portal, added that same year, are in constant use.

(10) Elk Run culvert, built ca. 1894 or possibly earlier, remains in excellent condition.

(11) While not associated directly with the main stem, rubble from the piers for the original Wernwag-built pedestrian bridge, Wager's Bridge (ca. 1825), is visible at times of low water.

## Conclusion

At Harpers Ferry, the waters of the Potomac and the Shenandoah Rivers brought prosperity and helped inspire technological innovation, but their presence also brought ruin, both indirectly and directly. While water power attracted industries and the valley afforded canals and railroads a convenient pathway, these same characteristics brought the destruction of war and floods. The town could not fully recover from the recurrent destruction, and the fickleness of the river eventually drove businesses, factories, and the popu-

*Figure 12-A 1997 view along the B&O's river wall, with the armory grounds on the right. (IHTIA, photo by author.)*

lace from lower Harpers Ferry, never to return. By the early twentieth century the lower town was nearly deserted and the mills were in ruins. The population, which had peaked at nearly three thousand persons before the Civil War, dwindled to less than five hundred by 1930. In 1936, the C&O Canal, battered by floods and plagued with obsolescence, finally closed. Because of the historic significance of Harpers Ferry (relating John Brown's Raid and the Civil War) the National Park Service acquired stewardship of the historic lower town in 1933. Later, it also acquired the C&O Canal towpath.

The B&O no longer exists as a corporation, lost in a series of mergers in recent years. Beginning in 1961, the B&O was taken over by the Chesapeake and Ohio Railroad. After 1973, the B&O, C&O, and Western Maryland railroads were collectively called the Chessie System, although the B&O retained its identity. In 1980, the CSX Corporation was created with the merger of the Chessie System and the Seaboard Coast Line Industries. The B&O finally disappeared as a corporation name in 1987, fully consolidated into CSX Transportation, one of the country's

largest railroads.[7]  Ironically, of all the
early industries at Harpers Ferry, the railroad is the only one still active, a fact that
can only add to this location's importance.  During its existence, the B&O (and
now CSX) has reflected nearly the entire
history of railroads in the New World.
While the bridges built at Harpers Ferry
spanned waters, they have also spanned
time, and can carry us to the past should
we care to cross.

## Notes

1.  Downs, *Who's Who in Engineering*, 75.

2.  Baltimore and Ohio Railroad, Drawing 3191, "Bridge
40," 1931.

3.  Ibid.

4.  Roberts, *East End*, 30.

5.  Ibid.

6.  Ibid., 32.

7.  Jacobs, *The History of the Baltimore & Ohio*, 127.

# Bibliography

## Published Sources

Aler, F. Vernon. *Aler's History of Martinsburg and Berkeley County, West Virginia.* The Mail Publishing Company, Hagerstown, Maryland, 1898.

Anonymous. *Annual Reports of the President and Directors to the Stockholders of the Baltimore & Ohio Railroad.* Baltimore, 1827-1962.

_____. *Baltimore & Ohio Railroad, Standard Plans for Maintenance of Way and Construction.* A. McKinnon Co., Inc., Cuyahoga Falls, Ohio, 1977.

_____. *Photographic Views of the Baltimore and Ohio Rail Road and its Branches, From the Lakes to the Sea.* Hagadorn Bros., Baltimore, 1872.

Baer, Christopher T. *Canals and Railroads of the Mid-Atlantic States, 1800-1860.* Regional Economic History Reearch Center, Eleutherian Mill-Hagley Foundation, Inc., Wilmington, Delaware, 1981.

Bushong, Millard. *Historic Jefferson County.* Carr Publshing Company Inc., Boyce, Va., 1972.

Calhoun, Daniel Hovey. *The American Civil Engineer: Origins and Conflict.* M.I.T., 1960.

Callahan, James Morton. *Semi-Centennial History of West Virginia.* Semi-Centennial Commission of West Virginia, 1913.

Condit, Carl. *American Building Art: The Nineteenth Century.* Oxford University Press, New York, 1960.

Conway, Martin. *Harpers Ferry, Time Remembered.* Carabelle Books, Reston, Va., 1981.

Darnell, Victor. *A Directory of American Bridge-Building Companies, 1840-1900.* Society for Industrial Archeology, Smithsonian Institution, Washington, D.C., 1984.

Dilts, James. *The Great Road, The Building of the Baltimore & Ohio, The Nation's First Railroad, 1828-1855.* Stanford University Press, 1993.

Downs, Winfield Scott, ed. *Who's Who in Engineering, A Biographical Dictionary of The Engineering Profession.* Lewis Historical Publishing Company, Inc. New York City, 1937.

Drinker, Henry. *Tunneling, Explosive Compounds, and Rock Drills.* John Wiley & Sons, New York, 1888.

Evans, Willis. *History of Berkeley County, West Virginia.* Willis Evans, 1928.

Frey, Robert, ed. *Railroads in the Nineteenth Century.* Bruccoli Clark Layman Co., New York, 1988.

Gilbert, Dave. *Where Industry Failed--Water Powered Industry at Harpers Ferry West Virginia.* Pictorial Histories Publishing Company, Charleston, WV., 1984.

Harwood, Herbert. *Impossible Challenge, The Baltimore and Ohio Railroad in Maryland.* Barnard, Roberts & Co., Inc., Baltimore, 1979.

Haupt, Herman. *General Theory of Bridge Construction.* D. Appleton and Co., New York, 1851.

Hayden, Martin. *The Book of Bridges.* Galahad Books, New York, 1976.

Henry, Robert. *This Fascinating Railroad Business.* The Bobbs-Merril Co., New York, 1942.

_____. *The Story of the Baltimore & Ohio Railroad, 1827-1927.* G.P. Putnam's Sons, New York, 1928.

Jacobs, Timothy, ed. *The History of the Baltimore & Ohio.* Crescent Books, New York, 1989.

Johnson, Emory. *Elements of Transportation.* Originally published in 1909, reprinted by Kennikat Press, Port Washington, New York, 1970.

Kirby, Richard Shelton, et al. *Engineering In History.* McGraw-Hill Book Company, Inc., New York, 1956.

Kirby, Richard Shelton, and Philip Gustave Laurson. *The Early Years of Modern Civil Engineering.* Yale University Press, New Haven, 1932.

Lee, Antoinette, et al. *A Biographical Dictionary of American Civil Engineers.* Committee on History and Heritage of American Civil Engineers, American Society of Civil Engineers, New York, 1972.

Long, Stephen. *Description of the Jackson Bridge*, Baltimore, 1830.

McDonald, Hunter, et al. *The Civil Engineer: His Origins.* Committee on History and Heritage of American Civil Engineers, American Society of Civil Engineers, New York, 1970.

Plowden, David. *Bridges, The Spans of North America.* Viking Press, New York, 1974.

Poor, Henry Varnum. *History of the Railroads and Canals of the United States of America.* New York, 1860.

Reizenstein, Milton. *The Economic History of the Baltimore and Ohio Railroad, 1827-1853.* Johns Hopkins Press, Baltimore, 1897.

Ringwalt, John L. *Development of Transportation Systems in the United States.* Published by author, Philadelphia, 1888.

Roberts, Charles. *East End.* Barnard, Roberts and Co., Inc., Baltimore, 1992.

Rubin, Julius. *Canal or Railroad? Imitation and Innovation in the Response to the Erie Canal in Philadelphia, Baltimore, and Boston.* The American Philosophical Society, Philadelphia, 1961.

Sagle, Lawrence, and Alvin Staufer, ed. *B&O Power, Steam Diesel and Electric Power of the Baltimore and Ohio Railroad, 1829-1964.* Standard Printing and Publishing Co., Carrollton, Ohio, 1964.

Savage, Christopher. *An Economic History of Transportation.* Hutchinson and Co. Ltd., London, 1959.

Schodek, Daniel. *Landmarks in American Civil Engineering.* M.I.T. Press, 1987.

Smith, William Prescott. *History and Description of the Baltimore and Ohio Railroad.* John Murphy & Co., Baltimore, 1853.

_____. *The Book of the Great Railway Celebrations of 1857.* D. Appleton & Co., New York, 1858.

_____. *The B&O in the Civil War: From the Papers of William Prescott Smith.* Edited by William Bain. Sage Books, Denver, 1966.

Snell, J.B. *Early Railways.* Octopus Books, London, 1972.

Stover, John. *History of the Baltimore & Ohio Railroad.* Purdue University Press, West Lafayette, Indiana, 1987.

Summers, Festus. *The Baltimore and Ohio in the Civil War.* G.P. Putnam's Sons, 1939.

Tyrell, Henry. *History of Bridge Engineering.* Tyrell Publishing, Chicago, 1911.

Urquhart, Leonard, and Charles O'Rourke. *Design of Steel Structures.* McGraw-Hill Book Company, New York, 1930.

Van Metre, Thurman. *Trains, Tracks, and Travel.* Simmons-Boardman Publishing Corporation, New York, 1926.

Weitzman, David. *Traces of the Past.* Charles Scribner's Sons, New York, 1980.


## Journal, Newspaper, and Magazine Articles

Adams, William Bridges. "The Construction and Duration of the Permanent Way of Railways in Europe." *Transactions of the American Society of Civil Engineers,* Volume XI, 244-298.

Anonymous. "A Mile Stone in Bridge Design." *Railway Age,* Volume 77, No. 4, July 26, 1924, 138.

_____. "Artists' Excursion Over the Baltimore and Ohio Rail Road." *Harpers New Monthly Magazine,* Volume XIX, June, 1859, 1-19.

_____. "Jonathan Knight: First Chief Engineer of the Baltimore and Ohio Railroad. *Baltimore and Ohio Railroad Employees Magazine,* Volume 5, No. 5, September, 1917, 18-20.

_____. "Subways for Safety." *Baltmore and Ohio Railroad Employees Magazine,* Volume 1, No. 8, May, 1913.

_____. "The Late Wendel Bollman." *The Railroad Gazette,* March 14, 1884, 200.

_____. *Virginia Free Press,* Martinsburg, West Virginia, 1835-1843.

Bush, H.D, et al. "Discussion on American Railroad Bridges." *Transactions of the American Society of Civil Engineers,* Volume XXI, December, 1889, 566-607.

Cooper, Theodore. "American Railroad Bridges." *Transactions of the American Society of Civil Engineers,* Volume XXI, No. 418, July, 1889, 1-59.

DeLony, Eric. "The Golden Age of the Iron Bridge." *American Heritage of Invention & Technology,* Fall 1994, Volume 10, No. 2, 8-22.

Gray, George. "Notes on Early Practice in Bridge Building." *Transactions of the American Society of Civil Engineers,* Volume XXXVII, June, 1897, 1-16.

Greiner, J.E. "The American Railroad Viaduct, Its Origin and Evolution." *Transactions of the American Society of Civil Engineers,* Volume XXIV, October, 1891, 349-361.

Horvath, Thomas. "Railfanning West Virginia's Ten-Mile Triangle, Part I: Harpers Ferry, West Virginia." *Railpace Magazine,* December, 1992, 16.

Ketzner, R.L. "Bridge 64, Cumberland Division." *Baltimore and Ohio Magazine,* February, 1928, Volume 15, No. 10, 127.

Lang, Philip George. "Old Bollman Truss Bridges on the Valley R.R. of Virginia." *Engineering News-Record,* Volume 90, No. 15, 672-673.

_____. "Bridge 64, Cumberland Division, a Fine Example of the Bollman Truss Structure." *Baltimore and Ohio Magazine,* Volume 15, No. 8, December, 1927, 7.

_____. "B. & O. Replaces Bridges of Historic Interest." *Railway Age,* Volume 77, No. 4, 145-148.

Schneider, Charles C. "The Evolution of the Practice of American Bridge Building." *American Society of Civil Engineers Transactions,* Volume LIV, June, 1905, 213-234.

Sisson, William Lee. "Harpers Ferry Improvement." *Transactions of the American Society of Civil Engineers,* Volume XXXII, October, 1894, 351-362.

Taylor, W.D.  "Pioneer Railway Development in the United States."  *Transactions of the American Society of Civil Engineers,* Volume LXXIV, December, 1911, 95-165.

Thatcher, Edwin.  "Description of a Combined Triangular and Suspension Bridge Truss, and Comparison of its Cost With That of the Warren, Pratt, Whipple and Howe Trusses."  *Transactions of the American Society of Civil Engineers,* Volume XIII, May, 1884, 123-158.

Vogel, Robert M.  "Speculations on the History and Original Appearance of the Last Bollman Truss."  *IA-The Journal of the Society for Industrial Archeology,* Volume 7, 1970, 425-438.

_____.  "The Engineering Contributions of Wendel Bollman."  *Contributions from the Museum of History and Technology:  Paper 36,* 1964, 79-104.


## Unpublished Sources

Bollman, Wendel.  "Construction of Bridges."  United States Patent Office, Patent No. 8,624, January 6, 1852.

Comp, T. Allan, and Donald Jackson.  "Bridge Truss Types: A Guide to Dating and Identifying."  American Association for State and Local History Technical Leaflet, no date.

CSX Corporation.  "Maryland Division Roadway Maps, Lines Between Weverton and Cumberland, Maryland, Cumberland Sub-Division."  August, 1981.

CSX Corporation.  "Track Charts, Baltimore, Maryland, to Fairmont, West Virginia."  Circa 1989.

Fink, Albert.  "Bridge."  United States Patent Office, Patent No. 10887, May 9, 1854.

Kemp, Emory.  "West Virginia's Historic Bridges."  The West Virginia Department of Culture and History, West Virginia Department of Highways, and the Federal Highway Administration, May, 1994.

Snell, Charles W.  "Historic Building Site Survey Report for Wager Lot No. 1 & the Bridge Lot, The Baltimore and Ohio Railroad Company's Bridge and Building at Harpers Ferry."  Harpers Ferry National Historic Park, National Park Service, Department of the Interior, September 22, 1958.

_____.  "The Business Enterprises and Commercial Development of Harpers Ferry's Lower Town Area, 1803 to 1861."  Harpers Ferry National Historic Park, National Park Service, Department of the Interior, April 9, 1973.

Stinson, D.E.  "The First Railroad Bridge at Harpers Ferry."  Harpers Ferry National Historic Park, National Park Service, Department of the Interior, March 10, 1970.

Wernwag, Lewis.  "Truss Bridge."  United States Patent Office, Patent No. 5760x, December 22, 1829.

Williamsport Historic Preservation Training Center.  "B&O railroad Bridge Piers Stabilization Design Project."  Harpers Ferry National Historical Park, National Capital Region, Assessment Data and Treatment Recommendations Report, May 6, 1994.


## Collections

Frank Duff McEnteer Collection.  The Institute for the History of Technology and Industrial Archaeology, Eberly College of Arts and Sciences, West Virginia University, Morgantown, West Virginia.

Harpers Ferry Photo Collection.  Harpers Ferry National Historic Park, Harpers Ferry, West Virginia.

Harpers Ferry Photo Collection. West Virginia and Regional History Collection, West Virginia University, Morgantown, West Virginia.

Interstate Commerce Commission Records, Railroad Valuation Reports. "Baltimore and Ohio Railroad Bridging Notes, Tunnel Notes, and Structure Notes." Record Group 134, National Archive, Washington, DC.

Thomas Hahn Collection. The Institute for the History of Technology and Industrial Archaeology, Eberly College of Arts and Sciences, West Virginia University, Morgantown, West Virginia.